FINDERS
KEEPERS

EMILY RODDA

FINDERS KEEPERS

Illustrated by NOELA YOUNG

HARCOURT BRACE & COMPANY

Orlando   Atlanta   Austin   Boston   San Francisco   Chicago   Dallas   New York

Toronto   London

This edition is published by special arrangement with Greenwillow Books, a division of William Morrow & Company, Inc.

Grateful acknowledgment is made to Greenwillow Books, a division of William Morrow & Company, Inc. for permission to reprint *Finders Keepers* by Emily Rodda, illustrated by Noela Young. Text copyright © 1990 by Emily Rodda; illustrations copyright © 1990 by Noela Young.

Printed in the United States of America

ISBN 0-15-302190-X

3 4 5 6 7 8 9 10   011   97 96 95 94

For Narelle Spencer, with love

CONTENTS

1
Beginnings

"Patrick, turn that TV off! Patrick, are you in there?"

Patrick stayed where he was. His mother sounded hassled—up to her ears in supermarket shopping in the kitchen while his little brother fussed around her, "helping." With a bit of luck she wouldn't call out again and he'd get another ten minutes of peace.

Not that there was anything worth watching. You'd think they'd try a bit harder on Saturday morning. He carefully aimed the remote control and flicked through the channels. Sport, sport, test pattern, old black-and-white movie, snow, snow . . . a quiz program—that was more like it, but it wasn't on a proper channel— some out-of-town station probably—bad luck.

He squinted at the spotty, jumping picture on the screen. A quizmaster with a bow tie and a mustache introduced a confused-looking contestant.

"Patrick, d'you want to see what I found at the mall? Can I watch my video? Will you put on Mickey now?" His little brother was hanging around the door, eating a cookie.

"No, Danny. Not now. I'm watching," said Patrick impatiently.

Danny screwed up his eyes and took a breath. Patrick put his hands over his ears and stubbornly stared straight ahead. On the blurry TV screen the round-faced quizmaster opened his mouth and laughed. In Patrick's living room, four-year-old Danny opened his mouth and roared.

"Patrick! What's happening in there?" Dimly Patrick heard his mother's voice, over Danny's yells and the roaring from the TV, and through his hands. She must have reached screeching point. He eased the fingers

covering his right ear. He'd better do something fast, or there'd be trouble. He sighed and walked over to the TV.

"Don't cry, Danny," he said in a kind, reasonable, loud voice. "I'll put on your video, okay?"

He pushed a few buttons. The grinning quizmaster was cut off in midgiggle.

"You said you wouldn't put Mickey on!" protested Danny. "You said—"

"No, I didn't."

"Yes, you did."

"No, I didn't."

"Patrick!" howled the voice from the kitchen.

Patrick sighed again and pushed the last button. Danny's video began its twenty-eighth run, and Danny retreated to the couch, his eyes fixed to the screen.

"I was watching something, you know," mumbled Patrick, suddenly angry again. He felt unloved and hard done by. He went over to a chair and curled himself up into a ball. He began to imagine that he was being held prisoner by a hideous monster with three eyes and slimy green tentacles. He couldn't move. He struggled against the invisible web that bound him. He had to get free. He writhed and butted his head against the chair back, grunting with effort.

"Patrick!"

He slowly raised his head. Judith, his mother, was standing over him, her hands on her hips. She was shaking her head.

"Patrick, I've told you and I've told you. Don't be rough on that chair! It's on its last legs already."

Patrick guiltily slid his feet to the floor and unclenched his fists. He regarded the old armchair gloomily. It was big and comfortable and just the right size for curling up in, but there were already darns and patches on the arms, and in other places the threads of the covering were worn thin and you could see the stuffing underneath getting ready to burst through.

"Sorry, Mum," he mumbled. "I forgot."

"Well, don't forget!"

"You forgot about my new sneakers." Patrick decided that the best means of defense was attack. "You said last Saturday we'd get them this Saturday. And you forgot."

Judith clasped her hand to her forehead. "I did!" she groaned. "I clean forgot. Oh, dear—you could have reminded me, Patrick!"

"Sshhh," hissed Danny from the couch.

"Oh, pardon me!" exclaimed Judith, but she lowered her voice. "Well, you'll just have to manage till next week, Patrick. I'll get your father to mind Danny and we'll go next Saturday morning. Okay? I just couldn't face Chestnut Tree Village again today. It's a madhouse."

"Mum! Have you seen my sunglasses?" Patrick's older sister, Claire, strode into the room. "They were in the kitchen and now they're gone! Someone's taken them."

"No one's taken them, Claire. And what were they doing in the kitchen anyway? No wonder you're always losing things." Judith shook her head and went back to the kitchen.

"I didn't lose them," Claire shouted after her. "I put them there so I'd know where they were. And I've got to go to my piano lesson now. I'll go blind if I have to go out in that sun without my sunglasses."

"I saw them," volunteered Patrick. "They're on the kitchen counter."

Claire stamped her foot and tossed her hair back. "They're not!" she fumed. "Someone's moved them." Her eyes narrowed. "I bet you did, Patrick. I bet you were playing with them. Where are they? You'd better not have broken them."

Patrick lost his temper. "I didn't touch your stupid sunglasses," he yelled. "They're on the stupid kitchen counter. I saw them, stupid!"

"Stupid yourself!"

"Stop fighting!" roared Judith from the kitchen. "Claire, come here."

"I can't *hear*!" shouted Danny from the couch.

"Mum, Patrick's taken my sunglasses," cried Claire passionately. "He's always taking my things. One of my best, *best* earrings has gone, too. You know, the stripy ones Julia gave me? He's a little pest! He's—oh."

Judith stood in the doorway, arms folded. She was wearing a pair of sunglasses.

"Where were they?" Claire exclaimed.

"On the kitchen counter, in plain sight. Why don't you look!" sighed her mother, pulling off the sunglasses and tossing them to her.

"They weren't there," Claire mumbled stubbornly.

"Well, obviously they were," said Judith dryly, going back to the kitchen. "Now, get off to your piano lesson and watch out for the traffic."

"And say you're sorry to me," chipped in Patrick. "Because I didn't take them, did I?"

"It's usually you," retorted Claire. "And what about my earring? I saw you looking at them. Now you've gone and lost one. Pest!" She turned and went out of the room. "Bye, Mum!" she shouted from the hall, and the front door slammed.

"She's the pest," muttered Patrick. "I never touched her stupid earring." He punched the back of the chair viciously. With a soft little sigh, the material split like a sausage under his knuckles, and a lump of white filling burst through. He stared at it, aghast.

Danny turned his head to look. His eyes widened with delight, and he scrambled from the couch. "Hey, Mum," he laughed. "Look what Patrick found in the chair! White stuff!"

"What!" The voice from the kitchen was furious.

With a sinking heart Patrick heard the mother-is-on-the-warpath footsteps approaching. This was not turning out to be a very good day.

2
THE INVITATION

After school on Monday Patrick walked home as usual from the bus stop with his friend Michael.

"What would you do if you had a million dollars?" he said. It was one of their favorite questions.

"Buy a Ferrari," Michael answered instantly.

Patrick nodded. Michael always said that. Or at least he always said he'd buy some car or other. Sometimes it was a Jag, sometimes a Mercedes. Today it was a Ferrari.

"What would you?" asked Michael carelessly.

"A computer," said Patrick firmly. "I'd buy a really great computer, and lots of games. And then I'd buy a house for myself to live in, that was mine. With my own TV, and my own chairs, and an elevator, and a swimming pool, and a garden. And no one could come in unless I said."

Michael shrugged. "A Ferrari's better," he said

flatly. He had a computer already. And as for the rest, he was an only child and no one got in his way at home.

They went on talking about cars after that, but when Michael had turned off down his own street Patrick started thinking again about the house he'd have if he had a million dollars.

It would all be new—new chairs, new paint on the walls, new carpets—everything clean and bright and new. Nothing that had to be mended, like the old chair that Mum had had to fix on Saturday. The tear he'd made in the cover was only small, but she'd got out her workbasket and stitched it up straightaway—well, almost straightaway. She'd yelled at him for quite a while first.

"A stitch in time saves nine," she said, sucking at the cotton to make it stiff so she could thread the needle. "That's an old saying. It means it's easier in the long run to fix something as soon as you can. If you leave it, the tear gets bigger and bigger so it's much harder to mend. Now, Patrick, I beg of you, keep out of this chair. Please, darling. Try to remember." He'd apologized, and promised. Again.

He came to the last little group of shops before his own turnoff. His mother complained that they weren't useful shops at all. One sold office furniture. The one next door to it used to be a dry cleaners but had been shut up for a long time. Then there was a real estate agent, with lots of pictures of houses in the window. So far, Patrick agreed with Judith. But the fourth shop was a very different matter, because it sold computers, and to Patrick it was the most interesting shop in the whole street—by a very long way. If—when—he got his own computer, it would be very handy to have a place so close to home where he could buy extra games and get advice. And in the meantime. . . .

He pressed his nose against the window and looked in, as he did almost every afternoon. The man who owned the shop was huddled over a computer in one corner, talking hard to a woman and a girl in school uniform. Patrick wrinkled his nose enviously. There was a kid who was in luck.

He slipped into the doorway, stuck his hands in his pockets, and wandered casually down the rows of gleaming gray machines, looking for one that was switched on. Sometimes the computer man got cranky if he caught you playing with the stock. If he thought you weren't a customer, that is, and he'd given up on Patrick long ago. But today he'd probably be too busy making a sale to complain.

In the middle of the back row one of the machines was quietly humming to itself. Patrick sat down in front of it and smiled gleefully. A game program! So he was in luck, too. He chose the game called "Quest" and settled down to play, hunching quietly over the keyboard. It was some sort of treasure hunt. A little figure on the screen was walking through rooms, and you could control which way it went. There was a scoreboard in one corner. That must be where the treasure you found was written up. Patrick frowned in concentration. He wanted to find one thing at least before the computer man finished with his customers and threw him out.

The little figure on the screen trotted through a doorway. "Come on!" Patrick whispered. He wished he'd been able to read the instruction book. There must be clues to where in this maze the treasures were. Then he noticed a slight break in one of the walls. He drove his figure straight to it—and yes! A little chest piled with jewels flashed into the scoreboard. Success!

The computer gave a sharp pinging sound. Patrick looked anxiously over at the group in the corner. The shop owner glanced at him but didn't say anything, turning back instead to his customers with a gracious

smile. Relieved, Patrick looked back to the screen and jumped. It had gone completely black, except for three words flashing in the middle.

WHO ARE YOU?

Patrick hesitated.

WHO ARE YOU?
WHO ARE YOU?
WHO ARE YOU?

flashed the computer.

Patrick shrugged. He hadn't read the instruction book, and he didn't know the right answer.

Oh, well. PATRICK, he typed, just for the fun of it, and waited for the GAME OVER sign to appear.

But it didn't. And he watched in amazement as something else did.

CONGRATULATIONS PATRICK!
YOU ARE NOW INVITED
TO COMPETE IN FINDERS KEEPERS
THE MILLION-DOLLAR TV GAME SHOW

FABULOUS PRIZES!

YOU'RE CHOSEN BY CHANCE
AND YOU TAKE YOUR CHANCE
IN FINDERS KEEPERS

DO YOU ACCEPT THE INVITATION?

YES, typed Patrick carefully. What a great game! He'd never seen anything like this before.

The computer screen went black again, and he waited impatiently. But when more words finally appeared, he stared at them, baffled.

TURN TO CHANNEL 8
AT 10 A.M. SATURDAY
TO MEET YOUR HOST
LUCKY LANCE LAMONT
AND PLAY FINDERS KEEPERS

UNDERSTOOD?

Patrick's mouth fell open. This didn't seem like part of a game.

The computer gave another sharp ping, and the last word on the screen started flashing.

UNDERSTOOD? UNDERSTOOD? UNDER . . .

"What are you doing over there, son?" asked the computer man with a menacing smile. He said something to the woman and half rose from his seat.

YES, Patrick typed rapidly.

The screen flashed, the computer hummed loudly. Eyes wide, Patrick jumped up from his chair as the man strode, grumbling, toward him.

"Just looking," gabbled Patrick, making for the door. "Sorry."

He ran out of the shop and down the street. He ran all the way to his own front gate. He had to tell someone about this.

He rang the bell, panting. He heard soft, trotting footsteps, and with a little lurch of disappointment remembered that his mother wasn't home. It was Monday, the day Estelle came to baby-sit while Judith was working.

The door opened a crack and a nose advanced cautiously, followed by two nervous pale blue eyes. As soon as they saw him, the eyes lost their frightened look. "Oh, Patrick, it's you, dear heart," twittered Estelle. She shut the door again and the door chain rattled. Patrick waited impatiently. Estelle was afraid of burglars, so she always kept the door chain on. The trouble was, she always got in a tangle when the time came to get the door open.

"Come in out of the heat, Patrick." Smiling her sweet, timid smile, Estelle swung the door open at last. "Did you have a good day? My word, you look hot! Have you been running? You really shouldn't. . . ."

Patrick gulped, swallowed, and grabbed her arm, stopping her in midflutter. "Estelle!" he gasped. "You'll never believe what just happened!"

Estelle looked at him in alarm.

"Nothing bad," he quickly assured her. "At the computer shop. I got the chance to go in a game. I think. I mean, I got invited. . . ." His voice trailed off. Estelle smiled at him kindly, her pale face and light, wispy hair hovering above him in the dimness of the hall.

"That's nice, Patrick," she said, nodding encouragingly. "A new game, is it? You love those computer games, don't you?"

"No, Estelle, it wasn't a game. At least, it was at first, but then. . . . It was—like a message. To me. With my name." Patrick couldn't believe how hard this was to explain.

"Oh, well, isn't that marvelous? The things they think of!" exclaimed Estelle, taking his schoolbag and putting it neatly on the hall stand. "How about a nice drink, now, dear heart? Come on."

She wafted off in the direction of the kitchen. Patrick trailed after her. He should have known it would be no good trying to tell Estelle. He'd have to wait till someone else came home. He pressed his hands together. They were trembling. His heart was beating fast, not just from running. Every time he thought about the message, it gave a hard flutter that made him catch his breath. Especially when he thought about the very last words that had flashed up on the screen before it went black and he ran from the shop.

SEE YOU SATURDAY!

3

"Nobody Listens to Me!"

For the rest of the afternoon Patrick thought about the message. *You are now invited to compete in Finders Keepers . . . Channel 8 . . . 10 A.M. Saturday.* He wrote the words down carefully, as he remembered them. He shivered as he finished. *Understood? . . . See you Saturday!*

At five o'clock a key turned in the front door lock and the door slammed open against the chain.

"Estelle!" called Claire through the crack, and Patrick heard Estelle let her in. Claire's feet pounded up the stairs. Patrick went to his door and peeped out at her.

"Hi, Patrick," she said cheerfully, and disappeared into her bedroom, which was beside his own. She kicked the door shut. Her schoolbag thumped to the floor and music began to beat through the wall.

Patrick made a decision. This was too big a thing to

handle on his own, and Claire seemed to be in a good mood. He'd talk to her about it. He picked up the piece of paper on which he'd written down the message and walked slowly to her door, thinking about what he'd say. He pushed the door open.

"Patrick, get out of here! I'm changing!" Claire, in her underwear, clutched her school uniform to her chest and frowned at him furiously.

"I want to tell you something," mumbled Patrick.

"Tell me later," she said impatiently. She turned her back on him and pulled on some shorts and a T-shirt. The music blared. Patrick tried to gather his thoughts.

"I've got to go on a TV show," he said loudly.

Claire spun around, her face alive with interest. "TV? What do you mean?"

Now he had her. Now came the hard part.

"See, I got this message," said Patrick gruffly, waving his piece of paper. "On a computer. Up on the screen. It said—"

Her face fell. "Oh, sure!" she groaned, and rolled her eyes. She sat down on the bed.

"It's true!" urged Patrick. "It said I'd been chosen by chance. For 'Finders Keepers'—that's the show. A million-dollar show. On Channel 8. It said—"

"Oh, sure, Patrick! There's no such show. And there's no such channel here."

"There is so!" shouted Patrick desperately, over the pounding music. "There must be. On Saturday. It said—"

"Look, will you get out of here? You're not allowed in my room."

Patrick stared at her, baffled and angry. "Claire, why don't you listen to me?" he said. "I'm not lying—I'm telling you. . . ."

"Claire!" Estelle's voice floated up the stairs. "Julia on the phone for you."

"Okay!" Claire bounded up, pushed past Patrick, and left the room. He heard her jumping down the stairs two at a time.

He stamped back to his own room and climbed onto his bed, throwing the message onto the desk. Well, that hadn't been much help, had it? He should have known she wouldn't believe him. Well, on Saturday she'd be sorry. She'd get a big shock then, wouldn't she? *Fabulous prizes.* She'd get a shock when he got some fabulous prizes from being on "Finders Keepers." All he had to do was wait.

ON TUESDAY, on the bus, Patrick told Michael about "Finders Keepers." Michael was as disbelieving as Claire had been. He got quite angry, in fact. He reminded Patrick of the time Patrick had convinced him that the street trees were powered by batteries.

"I was just kidding then, Michael," protested Patrick.

"Well, I believed you, didn't I? And I told Dad and he said you were telling me stories and I was a silly dope to believe you. Well, I'm not a silly dope now and I don't believe you now. So give up." He hunched his shoulders and turned away to stare out the window.

ON WEDNESDAY, as he ate his breakfast, Patrick asked his mother about Channel 8. He didn't mention the computer or "Finders Keepers." He'd had enough of trying to convince people about that.

"There's no such channel in this city, darling," said Judith, stuffing peanut butter sandwiches and apples into lunch boxes with reckless speed. "Eat up. Danny, don't do that with your milk. Danny? Danny! Oh, you naughty boy!" She dived for the dishcloth.

Danny watched, fascinated, as his milk spread in a glistening white pool on the tabletop, reached the edge, and began to stream in a miniwaterfall to the floor.

"Why isn't there?" asked Patrick.

"Well, there just isn't. No one broadcasts on that channel here, that's all," said Judith, from under the table. "Patrick, get me some paper towels, will you? Oh, Danny, that was so silly!"

Danny looked at his empty cup and the still-dripping milk. His lip trembled.

"Maybe a channel might only work on certain days," said Patrick eagerly. He passed a wad of paper towels to her. "Do you think, Mum?"

"Do you know I haven't got a single pair of socks that match?" exclaimed Claire, walking into the room. "Oh, yuck! Who spilled the milk?"

"Who do you think?" muttered Judith darkly, getting to work with the towels.

Danny opened his mouth and cried. Tears fell down his cheeks. "My milk fell down!" he wept.

"Oh, dear, poor Danny," soothed Claire. "Never mind, darling. Claire will get you some more, okay? Stop crying now. It'll be all cleaned up in a minute."

There was a disgusted snort from Judith on the floor.

Patrick finished his breakfast and walked upstairs. His father, Paul, was shaving in the bathroom. The electric razor buzzed in a comforting, familiar sort of way.

"Dad?"

"Mmm?" His father screwed his mouth up and over to one side and mowed at his cheek.

"How do people get on TV quiz shows?"

"They write in and get picked, I suppose."

"Do they ever just ask people to go on?"

"They might, I guess. I really don't know, Patrick. Are you all ready for school?"

"Yes. Dad?"

"Mmm?"

"Why isn't there a Channel 8 in our city?"

"Well, one day there might be." Paul turned off the razor and smiled at him absentmindedly. "We'll talk about it later, eh? In fact, I've got a book about how TV works, somewhere. You can read all about it. It's really—"

"But, Dad. . . ."

"Not now, Patrick. It's not the time. We're late."

"We're all *late!*" shouted Judith from downstairs. "Patrick! Paul! Come on!"

"Judith, are any of my socks down there? I've got eight single ones and no pairs!" bawled Paul.

"I've got twelve single socks, Dad. I beat you!" laughed Claire.

"You're both hopeless nincompoops!" roared Judith. "Why don't you pair them before they go into the wash?"

"I do!" Claire and Paul both replied indignantly.

Patrick wandered downstairs and out onto the front

porch, to wait. "Nobody listens to me!" he said grimly. He sat on the doorstep and rested his chin on his knees.

"I listen." Danny plumped down beside him. He fumbled with the catches on his little schoolbag. "I'm taking my special thing I found at the mall for show-and-tell, Patrick. Do you want to see?"

Patrick shook his head. "Not now, Danny," he said firmly. "We're late."

ON THURSDAY afternoon Patrick sneaked again into the computer shop to play "Quest." Nothing happened. No message, no questions appeared on the screen, though this time he found three lots of treasure. He walked home feeling confused and flat. Monday afternoon's adventure had started to seem very unreal. He sat in his room and read the message through again and again. Was it real, or wasn't it? He didn't know what to think anymore.

ON FRIDAY it was raining. One day to go. Patrick checked Channel 8 on the TV set before school. Nothing. Just roaring snow. When he went up to check the message, it had been blown off his desk by the squally wind that was blowing through his window. Feeling a bit foolish, he picked it up and put it carefully away in a drawer. In this house things got lost easily, and he didn't want to lose this—yet.

4
AT CHESTNUT TREE VILLAGE

On Saturday Patrick woke up with a little shock, knowing that this was a special day. For a moment he couldn't think exactly why, and then, with an excited flutter of his stomach, he remembered. At ten o'clock today he was going to find out once and for all about "Finders Keepers." He got dressed more carefully than usual, went downstairs, and turned on the TV. Quickly he switched channels. Cartoons, cartoons, advertisement, man talking, snow, snow . . . and still nothing at all on Channel 8.

"Patrick, tune it in, darling, if you're going to watch." Judith wandered past with the newspaper under her arm and her eyes half-closed. She headed for the kitchen. Patrick turned off the TV and followed.

"What's for breakfast, Mum?"

"We'll see," Judith murmured vaguely, plugging in the electric kettle. She blinked sleepily at him and smiled. "You look nice, darling," she said. "You're all ready. But we can't go till eight-thirty at the earliest, you know. Nothing'll be open till then."

Patrick's stomach lurched. "We aren't going out, are we?" he asked anxiously.

She began to make the tea. "Don't say you've forgotten!" she said. "I promised you, last Saturday. Your new sneakers, remember?"

"Oh—oh, but I can't go out this morning, Mum. There's something I've got to watch on TV. At ten o'clock. I've got to! My sneakers'll be all right for another week," gabbled Patrick, panic-stricken.

Judith faced him, hands on hips. "Patrick," she said wearily, "it's all organized. Dad's going to look after Danny, and we're going to get your sneakers and some new T-shirts. You remember."

"But, Mum, I've got to watch—"

"Patrick, your shoes are a disgrace. They're falling off your feet. There's no way we're going to cancel this because of a TV show."

"But, Mum. . . . !"

"Patrick, I'm sorry, but forget it! We're going to the mall this morning, and that's all there is to it!"

THE CHESTNUT Tree Village shopping center was crowded and full of sound—people talking, music playing, and now and again an announcement over the loudspeaker system about a lost child or a special sale at one of the hundreds of shops that lined the glossy-tiled

plazas on four levels. Patrick trailed gloomily behind Judith as she walked to the escalator. The shoe box in its
plastic bag bumped against his leg. He growled to himself. He'd paid dearly for those new sneakers.

"Cheer up, droopy drawers," said Judith. "You're
not much fun to go shopping with. And you're the one
who scored new shoes, too. Come on! How important
can a TV show be, for goodness' sake? What was it?"

"Doesn't matter," Patrick mumbled.

"Oh, a laugh a minute, you are," she sighed. "Oh,
listen, Patrick, there it goes."

The famous Chestnut Tree Village clock was striking
the quarter hour. Patrick looked at his own watch. It
was two minutes fast. He adjusted it absently. The
Chestnut Tree Village clock was never wrong. A quarter
to ten. They'd never be home in time now.

"I think I'll have a cup of coffee before we go," said
Judith. "Why not? We're hardly ever out by ourselves
these days, are we, Patrick? We'll celebrate. We'll go to
Smithy's and then you can have a drink and watch the
clock strike ten. Wouldn't that be good?"

"Aw, Mum!" Patrick rolled his eyes. "I've seen it
thousands of times."

She glanced at him quickly and then looked away.
"Oh, yes," she said. "I've been spending too much time
with Danny, that's my trouble. He loves it. You used to
love it, too." She looked, for a moment, a bit sad.

He shrugged, feeling uncomfortable. Actually, he
did still quite enjoy watching the clock do its stuff on

the hour. It was just that he was in a bad mood. Especially when he thought about ten o'clock.

"Well. . . ." Judith stepped off the escalator and held out her hand to him. "I'm going to have a cup of coffee. Why don't you drag yourself along with me and drown your sorrows? Come on, indulge me."

"Okay."

They sat down at one of the wooden tables outside the coffee shop and gave their orders. Patrick looked at the clock, which stood on a sort of platform, encircled by a little fence, near to where they sat. It was in the shape of a tree (a chestnut tree, of course) and under it stood the carved figure of a blacksmith, holding a huge hammer.

People were gathering, as usual, to watch the clock strike. In five minutes it would be ten o'clock. The clock would burst into life. The big figure of the blacksmith under the tree would begin pounding at the anvil with his hammer, to make the chimes. He did it for the half and quarter hours, too. Just one strike. But on the hour it was much more exciting. With every strike, birds would pop out of little doors all over the tree's branches and sing with wide open beaks, a smiling sun would peep from behind the green-painted leaves, and a squirrel would spring out of a hole in the trunk, waving its paws. It was the squirrel that Patrick always looked for.

Three minutes to go. Patrick sighed, caught his mother's eye, smiled crookedly, and looked away. The

"Finders Keepers" thing was silly, anyway. Everyone he'd talked to about it had said it couldn't be true. It must have been part of the "Quest" game after all.

"Nearly time," said Judith happily. She, at least, loved watching the clock, and she was enjoying her coffee.

Sipping his drink, Patrick looked idly around at the shops that lined the walls around them. He hadn't been up to this level for a while, and some of them had changed. Bookshop, bank, magic shop (he must remember that), antique shop, fancy tea and coffee shop, and all down one side the entrances to the top floor of the department store where they'd bought his T-shirts and shoes. Behind its big windows people wandered around looking at toasters and electric kettles and micro-

wave ovens, at CD players and speakers and radios, at stereos and VCRs and TV sets. . . .

TV sets! He sat up so fast that he nearly choked on his straw.

"Patrick?" Judith looked at him in alarm.

"I'm . . . I'll be back in a minute," he spluttered. "I want to . . . watch . . . from the other side. Okay, Mum? Okay?" He was already on his feet.

She shrugged in bewilderment. "Okay. But come straight back."

He tore away, slipping into the crowd, weaving through the people, making for those flickering screens behind the windows.

Through the big store's doorway . . . hurry, hurry! He could hear the clock beginning to whir behind him. There were seconds to go. Around the corner . . . down to the end of the bank of TV screens. He leaped for a dial—turned it—and as the blacksmith made his first strike, Channel 8 appeared on the screen before his eyes. He saw a grinning quizmaster, a giant wheel, a huge sign flashing.

The quizmaster opened his arms and laughed, straight into Patrick's eyes. "Patrick!" he shouted. "Are you ready to play . . . 'Finders Keepers'?"

Patrick's eyes bulged. He licked his lips, swallowed. "Yes," he squeaked.

"Well, come on over!" bawled the quizmaster.

And then everything went black.

5

Meet Lucky Lamont

There was a roaring noise in his ears. A velvety blackness pressed heavily against his eyes, pricked by hundreds of dancing points of light. He shook his head from side to side.

"Oh-oh, we've caught a little one this time, folks!" boomed a voice. "Think we should throw him back?"

Another sound rose up and mingled with the roaring noise. Laughter.

The voice boomed on. "Seriously, though, ladies and gentlemen, please put your hands together and welcome Patrick, our lucky Finder for today!"

There was a burst of applause. Patrick raised his head. Confusedly he realized that his own hands were blinding him, pressing against his eyes. He forced himself to relax—slowly, slowly. He opened his eyes and peeped through his fingers.

Bright lights, TV cameras, hundreds of people clapping and stamping and laughing—for him! His mouth dropped open.

The quizmaster leaned, grinning, toward him. His teeth flashed in the brilliant light. "That's the way, little pal. Relax! I won't bite you!"

Patrick shrank back. He wasn't so sure.

"Pat thinks we're crazy, crazy, crazy on this side of the Barrier!" hooted the quizmaster. "Are we crazy, folks?"

"*Yes!*" the audience roared with delight.

"But are we having fun?"

"YES!"

"All right! So let's tell Pat here all about us. What's my name?"

"Lucky Lance Lamont!" chorused the crowd.

"Right! And what's the game?"

"'FINDERS KEEPERS'!!" The audience howled, whistled, and stamped.

Patrick stepped quickly backward onto his own toe, stumbled, recovered, and blushed.

"Oh, he can dance, too! They're a talented lot over there," chortled Lucky. The audience roared. "Okay, okay, okay . . . so . . . ladies and gentlemen, it's 'Finders Keepers' time, and here she is, that lovely little lady, please welcome . . . Boopie . . . Cupid!"

A young woman in a short, shiny yellow dress with feathers on it tottered from behind the giant wheel to tumultuous applause. She had an enormous mane of blond curls, huge blue eyes, and a wide, white smile. She held out her arms to the delirious audience and shook her curls.

"Hi there, Boopie!" yelled Lucky. "Ready to spin that wheel?"

"Sure am, Lucky," smiled Boopie. She sparkled and glittered under the bright lights. Patrick stared at her, fascinated.

"Now, for Pat here, and for those people watching who haven't caught the show before, Boopie, now's the time to explain our game," cried Lucky, putting his arm around Patrick's shrinking shoulders. "Right, Pat?"

"Er . . . yeah," muttered Patrick, looking nervously at the TV cameras moving in on him.

"Yeah! So here we go!" Lucky led Patrick to one side of the studio. The camera people scrambled backward, heaving their cameras with them, following his every move.

Behind a long desk covered with silver question marks sat three very ordinary-looking people—an elderly woman wearing a lot of jewelry, a stern-faced man in a suit, and a plump younger woman with a freckled face and short, curly red hair. Patrick thought they looked at him in a rather disappointed sort of way, and he glanced warily at Lucky.

But Lucky was facing one of the cameras. A little frown had appeared on his face, and he was speaking earnestly, straight into the lens. From somewhere above his head soft, sad music had begun to play. The lights in the studio dimmed, but he was lit by a bright spotlight.

"Here are tonight's Seekers," crooned Lucky to the camera. "Their letters were chosen from the thousands we receive each and every week. They are here tonight on a very special quest." He paused. The audience was silent, and the sad music rose a little.

"These three people," Lucky continued, "have one thing in common. They have all lost something. Something very special to them. You've heard their stories, folks. You know they've tried their utmost to find the thing they've lost on our side of the Barrier. You know they've failed. And you know why."

The music began to rise, and Lucky's voice rose, too. Patrick stood rigidly to attention. His hands were sweating. He didn't understand any of this. What was this Barrier Lucky kept talking about? Who were these people?

"Our Seekers believe, and we agree with them, folks," Lucky was saying, "that their missing treasures have gone through the Barrier." He paused impressively. "They need a native from the other side to track them down. They need a Finder. We're going to give them one."

The music swelled. The audience burst into excited applause. Patrick blinked in the dimness. He felt a hand on his shoulder and a feather tickled his arm. "Get ready," breathed Boopie Cupid in his ear. He stiffened as she slipped away. Ready for what?

"Patrick!"

There was a blare of trumpets. Lucky swung around to face Patrick and jerked him into the spotlight. "You are our Finder, Patrick," he cried. "And here's what you can win!" He turned Patrick to face the huge wheel, now lit by another bright spotlight. Boopie stood beside it, her feathery yellow dress shining and her white teeth flashing.

"Tell us all about it, Boopie!" whooped Lucky.

"Well, Lucky, there's a fabulous range of prizes this week," trilled Boopie. "For the first Find, Patrick can win . . ." She held up her hand to the wheel and it began to spin. Pictures appeared on its whirling surface, and the audience started clapping and cheering. ". . . this superb set of diamond jewelry," cried Boopie, as a picture of necklaces, bracelets, and rings appeared. "Or"—the picture changed to one of a dark-gray computer—"this great Ezy-way computer with twelve different game programs, including the ever-popular 'Temple of Terror 2,' or. . . ." The picture changed again, to one of a set of garden tools, but Patrick could see nothing in his head but that computer. Imagine if he could win that! With all those games! For the first time since he'd begun this crazy adventure he felt really excited instead of just plain scared.

Boopie was still talking, and the pictures were still changing. Lounge chairs, statues, a music box with horses that went around and around, a mirror with a curly gold frame, golf clubs, a huge camping tent for four people, cameras, watches, clocks . . . the list went on and on, the pictures changed. Then at last the final picture disappeared and only the spinning wheel could be seen. "So, Patrick," said Boopie, turning to face him with a beaming smile, "any of these wonderful prizes could be yours today—when you play . . . 'Finders Keepers'!"

6
THE SEEKERS

"Right, Pat my friend, so now you know what you can win," beamed Lucky, squeezing Patrick's shoulder and twinkling at the audience. "Now we're going to see what you have to find. But first, we'll take a break for this message." He froze, smiling, for a moment, then the lights went on, the sound of an advertising jingle filled the air, and everyone started talking and running around. Lucky abruptly dropped his arm from Patrick's shoulder, and a girl in a pink smock trotted over to him and began patting a powder puff over his shiny red face.

Patrick looked around helplessly. If only he knew what he was supposed to do! That computer would really be worth winning. He'd like to see Claire's face when he. . . . Then he remembered his mother, and a stab of pure panic made him jump. She would be looking for him. Right now she'd be combing the shops and plazas of Chestnut Tree Village, panicking, thinking he'd been kidnapped or something.

A canary yellow figure appeared beside him and shook its curls. "Having fun, Patrick?" trilled Boopie Cupid.

Patrick opened his mouth and shut it again. Boopie didn't look to him as though she could decide on what to have for breakfast, let alone help him with a problem like this. But Lucky was having his jacket brushed now, and everyone else was racing around the place looking intent and busy and definitely not interested in him or his worries. He decided to try his luck.

"My . . . my mother will think I'm lost," he said to her awkwardly. "I didn't tell her—well, I didn't really know—that I was coming, see. I wasn't sure . . . and now, I. . . ." To his horror his voice failed, and his eyes began to prickle. He swallowed violently.

Boopie put her hand on his arm. "Don't worry, sweetie pie," she said seriously. "When you move across the Barrier this way, time more or less stands still for you. All being well, you'll be back on your side before your mum even notices you're gone."

"True?" The relief was enormous.

"Oh, yes. Don't worry. I'll make sure you're okay." She paused, and just for an instant the light died from her face, as though a shadow had crossed it. "I can do that, at least," she murmured. Then in a blink of an eye the smile was back. "So—that's settled," she beamed. "Now, are you clear on the game?"

"Well . . . sort of," Patrick said, glancing up at her nervously. "I have to find something, and if I do I win a prize. Like that computer."

"That's right, sugarplum. You've got it fine." Boopie flashed him another brilliant smile and turned to go. Desperately he caught at her arm. A bright yellow feather flew off her sleeve and floated to the ground. "Oh, sorry," he said.

"Never mind," she said gaily. "Lots more where that came from! Something else wrong? Be quick, the ad break's nearly over and I've got to get back to the wheel, sweetie pie. They like to record the show all in one go, you know. They don't like to have to cut out gaps afterward. The computer's been playing up, too, since—" She broke off abruptly and looked confused.

"What's the Barrier?" gabbled Patrick. "Where am I?"

"Ten seconds!" boomed a voice from the air. Boopie gave a little squeal. "Got to go. Tell you later. See you!" She whirled around and scuttled away, leaving another yellow feather in his hand. He blushed and shoved it into his jeans pocket, out of sight.

Lucky appeared at his side once more and adjusted his tie. The lights dimmed and the spotlight came on. "Four, three, two, one. . . ." boomed the voice, and then Lucky was speaking again.

"We're playing 'Finders Keepers,' the million-dollar game," he told the camera. "Now we're going to introduce Finder Patrick to our Seekers for tonight. And they're going to tell him just what they're looking for."

Suddenly he swung around to face the desk and the three people sitting there. A spotlight flashed onto the elderly woman on the left. She stared at Patrick with hollow gray eyes.

"What is your missing object, Eleanor Doon?" cried Lucky dramatically.

The woman dabbed at her lips with her handkerchief and began to speak in a high, cracked, singsong voice.

"My first is in fur but not in fun,
My second means just me alone,
My third is third as well in run,
My fourth begins my saddest groan.
I have three hearts of deepest red,
In shining gold they make their bed."

Patrick looked at her wildly. Was she crazy? What on earth did she mean?

"I must have it back," whispered Eleanor Doon, "I must." But Lucky quickly held up his hand. "Ah-ah-ah, Eleanor! No more clues. You know the rules," he said, shaking his head at her. She put her hand to her mouth. Her long, thin fingers were covered in expensive-looking rings, Patrick saw. Around her neck hung dozens of shining chains and necklaces. She must be very rich.

The spotlight moved to the man sitting in the middle. He stared out at the audience and the camera, stony-faced. He didn't look at Patrick.

"And what is your missing object, Clyde O'Brien?" demanded Lucky.

"A tree has died to give me birth,
But still I shelter feathered friends.
I'm large and heavy, colored earth,
With golden fringes my tail ends.
And where my name and others be,
My owner's name is plain to see."

The man delivered his message without a quiver. He didn't even blink while he was speaking. But Patrick noticed that his forehead was shiny with sweat. Was the spotlight making him hot? Or was he very, very nervous? Whichever it was, his poem didn't make any more sense to Patrick than Eleanor Doon's had. At this rate, there was no chance of getting that computer. Patrick turned to the last of the Seekers as the spotlight moved on. Maybe this one. . . .

"And our last Seeker, Wendy Minelli," said Lucky, throwing out his arm toward the freckled, redheaded young woman. "Wendy Minelli, what is your missing object?"

She smiled nervously at him and gave a little spluttering laugh.

"Um . . . I'm pink and bright . . . oh . . . um . . . sorry," she mumbled, blushing. "I'm a bit nervous."

"No need to be nervous, Wendy!" boomed Lucky, smiling fiercely. "Just go ahead. But we're running out of time, dear, so let's go!"

Patrick leaned forward, listening as hard as he could. He felt sorry for Wendy, and she had a nice face. He felt he would like to find whatever it was she'd lost, quite apart from any prize he might win.

"I'm . . . I'm pink and soft, with bright blue eyes," whispered Wendy Minelli.

"My ears are floppy, larger size,
Around my neck there is a bow,

So you can take me when you go.
And if you pull my yellow ring,
A song about a star I sing."

"Well, an easy one for you, Pat!" cried Lucky gaily.
"What do you think?"

Patrick nodded dumbly. It was true. This time he
could see what the rhyme might mean. Wendy's lost
treasure sounded as though it must be a child's soft
toy—probably a rabbit, if it had floppy ears that were
"larger size." A soft, pink rabbit with blue eyes and a
bow around its neck. And obviously it played a tune
when you pulled a string. Patrick had seen toys like that.

A smile crept across his face. The computer was
practically his. All he had to do now was get back home
and start looking. And at that thought the smile faded.
For, of course, he had no idea at all how or where to
start doing any such thing.

7

"Good Finding!"

"Okay!" Lucky clapped his hands together. "Now, Pat, our Seekers have written down their clues for you— Boopie!"

Boopie wobbled forward on her high heels, holding up a silver basket.

"Now, Pat, for the chance to win one of those wonderful prizes, choose your first Find!" Lucky pointed, beaming, to the basket. There was the roll of drums. The three Seekers leaned forward anxiously.

"But—um—can't I just decide which to find?" muttered Patrick.

Lucky laughed. "Oh, no, no! Not so easy, my friend. You're chosen by chance and you take your chance in 'Finders Keepers.' Isn't that right, folks?"

"Right!" yelled the audience delightedly.

The drums went on rolling. Boopie jiggled the basket invitingly above his head. Patrick closed his eyes, crossed his fingers for luck, stood on his toes, and plunged his arm into the basket. His fingers closed on a folded piece of paper and he pulled it out, hoping for the best. He unfolded it and read the message inside. "A tree has died to give me birth . . ." it began. Oh, no! He'd chosen the worst one of all!

Lucky, looking over his shoulder, crowed, "Clyde! Clyde O'Brien!" The audience began to cheer and clap.

The grim-faced man's mouth relaxed into what might have been a smile, for him. His hands gripped one another on the desktop. Patrick looked at the other two Seekers. Eleanor Doon's face was crumpled with disappointment, and Wendy Minelli's smile was so crooked that it was obvious she was nearly crying. He felt awful.

"Find Seeker Clyde's missing treasure, Pat, and you're a winner!" Lucky was shouting. "And you qualify to try for your second Find, and more great prizes!" He clapped Patrick on the back so hard that Patrick stumbled forward, almost knocking over Boopie Cupid and sending a whole cloud of yellow feathers flying. "Ah, there you go, you really have got dancing feet, haven't you, Pat? Shame Boopie's molting or she could join you. Ha, ha! Now, you pop off round the back with Boopie to get ready, and then you can be on your way." He turned back to the camera and the audience. "Okay, folks, he's on his way! Good Finding, Pat!"

"Good Finding!" roared the audience.

Rousing music began to play. Patrick ducked his head in embarrassment, pushed the piece of paper into his pocket, and let Boopie lead him away. As they passed the Seekers' desk, Wendy Minelli smiled anxiously at him and Eleanor Doon stared and bit her lip. Clyde O'Brien simply nodded, but again Patrick saw that his forehead was gleaming with perspiration. He tried to say something to Boopie, but she smiled and shook her curls and tripped gaily on, across the studio floor, past the great wheel, through a gap in the curtain behind it, and out a heavy door into an empty corridor.

Once the door had shut behind them, Boopie stopped and, with an enormous groan of relief, kicked off her shoes. "Oh, thank goodness, I didn't think I'd make it through," she wailed. "Oh, my dear, they were killing me!" She wriggled her toes and bent over, with difficulty, to rub them.

Patrick watched her awkwardly. After a few more moments of rubbing and sighing Boopie looked up at him through her curls. "Something wrong, sweetie pie?" she asked kindly.

"Ah—no!" he exclaimed. "It's just . . . I can't believe this is happening to me! I mean, Claire, that's my sister, and all of them, they all said it couldn't be true, and now . . ."

"Well, now you know Claire and all of them were talking through their pointy hats, don't you?" cried

Boopie. She grabbed his arm and padded quickly off along the corridor, pulling him with her past rows of green-painted doors.

"So," she said brightly, looking straight ahead. "You have a sister called Claire. I have a sister, too. She runs the cafeteria here. She's a wonderful cook. She's away at the moment, but she'll be back soon. Very soon, now. In fact, you'll probably meet her next week when you come back. Would you like that? She makes the best meat pies you've ever eaten, honestly. . . . Quickly, Patrick, let's hurry. . . . Now, what was I saying . . . oh, yes, the loveliest meat pies, do you like meat pies?"

Patrick was just concentrating on keeping up. Somehow he didn't think Boopie really wanted an answer. She seemed to be chattering about one thing while her mind was really occupied with something else. He wondered what it was.

The green-painted doors all looked exactly the same, but after a few minutes Boopie stopped at one, knocked three times, and went in, pulling Patrick behind her.

Patrick looked around. He was in a small, bare room, painted green like the door. There was a TV set hanging on one wall, a chair, a small cupboard. And in a corner, a thin, gray, tired-looking man punching away at a computer. Patrick saw with interest that it was an Ezy-way Plus 3, a jazzed-up version of the one on Boopie's prize wheel.

"Where've you been?" the man growled, without turning around.

Boopie shrugged. "Maxie, this is Patrick, the Finder. He's going for. . . ."

"I know, I know," grumbled the man. He scraped back his chair and stood up wearily. "Come on, we're running overtime as it is. We don't want any delays for this young chap. Especially the way this thing's acting at the moment. I can't work miracles, you know."

Boopie nibbled at her bright red lips. "Oh, we all know you can," she chattered nervously. "You're just tired, Max, that's your trouble. And we've got ages yet, really." She turned to Patrick.

"Now, look, sugarplum," she said. "I know you're confused, but everyone who plays is at first. There's really nothing to it. You just go back where you came from, and you find Mr. Whatsis—Clyde O'Brien, I mean—you find his lost thing. It's right in your neighborhood. All three things are."

"But—how do you know?" asked Patrick, feeling even more confused.

"Because Max has tracked them down there, of course," said Boopie patiently. "That's why your area got the invitation. That's why these three Seekers were chosen, if it comes to that. They only choose Seekers whose things Max can find."

Patrick stared at her. "So—you mean you already know where Mr. O'Brien's thing is?"

She shrugged. "More or less. Don't we, Max?"

The thin man grunted. He opened a red box that stood waiting beside him on the computer table and took something out. He stretched out his hand to Patrick. "Put this on," he said.

He was holding what looked like a brooch, with a small pearl at its heart.

"I'll do it, sweetie pie," said Boopie. "Don't want it to show, do we?" She quickly fastened the little brooch to the inside of Patrick's T-shirt, tickling his nose with her feathers. Patrick sneezed violently.

"Bless you!" said Boopie cheerfully. "Now, kidlet, when you hear that little gizmo start to go beep-beep-beep, like that, you know you're getting near what you're after—Mr. Whatsis's whatever-it-is, you know. Clever Max has set it so it'll do that. He's an absolute genius, Maxie is! A computer *genius*!" She hugged Max enthusiastically.

"Aw, talk sense, will you?" growled Max, and sneezed.

"I—I don't really understand, still," said Patrick hesitantly. "I'm sorry."

"Look, darling heart, it's really simple—" Boopie began, putting her hand on the computer. But Max cut in on her, firmly brushing the hand away.

"Don't *touch*, Boopie," he barked. "Don't you ever learn? And *I'll* explain it to him. He'd never understand you if he tried all week! It's a wonder to me that any of them ever do. And he's just a kid."

"Okay!" Boopie backed away and dropped down into Max's chair, looking suddenly pale and harassed. "But you'd better hurry up. We *are* getting late now." She turned her head away and began smoothing down her feathers. Patrick saw that her fingers were trembling and felt sorry for her. Max surely didn't have to be so crabby, however tired he was.

"Right. Now look," Max said to Patrick. "You've got to get it into your head first thing, that when you're here with us, you're in a different time stream from the one you're in when you're at home. Got that?"

Patrick nodded dumbly. He'd more or less accepted that already, though it seemed completely incredible.

Max nodded with satisfaction. "Right," he went on. "That's point one. Point two is that your time stream's separated from our time stream by the Barrier. It's like a wall. A very, very tall wall you can't get over, or under."

"It's just out there, actually," Boopie chipped in, gesturing vaguely over her shoulder. "Just down the road. That's why they built the studio here. Makes it easier to—"

"Boopie, what am I going to do with you!" growled Max, shaking his head at her. Then he relented and spoke more gently. "He doesn't need to know that, girl! That's where you always confuse them, going on like that!"

"Sorry," sighed Boopie. She went back to smoothing her feathers.

"For some reason, probably because on your side the Barrier's different from the way it is on ours, your people haven't worked out that it exists, or that we do, for that matter." Max sniffed in disgust. "It's beyond me why they haven't woken up to some extent, but obviously they haven't. Anyhow, we've always known about it, see. And over the years we've worked out that there are certain places where the Barrier's very weak. And you know what makes it weak? Something on your side. Go on, make a guess." He paused expectantly.

Patrick stared at him, openmouthed. "Mice?" he whispered.

Boopie snorted with laughter. Max frowned at her ferociously and she clapped a hand over her mouth.

"No, son," he said flatly. "Not mice. Clocks. The Barrier's always at its weakest in the general area of an especially big, powerful, chiming clock. Have you got anything like that near where you live? I'll bet you have."

Patrick nodded. "I sure do," he said. He'd always thought there was something special about the Chestnut Tree Village clock. Now he knew what it was.

Max nodded slowly. "It's always the same," he said to Boopie, then turned again to Patrick. "So, son," he went on, "are you following me? The Barrier has these weak spots, all along its length—"

"That's mostly where it breaks," Boopie put in, sitting forward in her chair.

"Breaks?" repeated Patrick slowly. This was becoming more and more incredible.

"Yes. It sort of tears—sometimes because it's had a knock or something, sometimes for no reason at all that we can see on our side. But anyway, then we have to fix it," Boopie explained brightly.

"Yes," droned Max, ignoring her, "but more to the point, before we can fix it, things tend to get sucked through to the other side—our side into your side, your side into our side. People and animals and such can't get through at all—not that way." He paused thoughtfully for a moment. "But things—well, they're another matter. Now, we're on the watch for Barrier breaks, so we don't lose that much, and when we get your stuff through, the Guards throw it back, if it's worth it, before the Department of Barrier Works team turns up to fix the hole."

"They don't bother throwing back lots of things," said Boopie seriously. "They're a lazy mob, those Barrier Guards, I reckon. I know one who told me. . . ."

"Single socks," said Patrick suddenly. "They wouldn't bother with those, would they?"

"Heavens no!" giggled Boopie. "Why do you ask that, sweetie pie? Lost some?"

"I know some people who have," grinned Patrick. He was starting to enjoy himself.

Max cleared his throat irritably. "Well, do you see the point, son? Every now and then, despite all the precautions and all, something someone really cares about goes through a hole in the Barrier, into your side. And there's nothing they can do about it."

"Except come to us," Boopie chipped in. "Because of Max's computer we can find their things—or at least . . ."

"What we can do," said Max, staring her into silence, "is locate them using the computer and then bring in Finders from the same general area, like yourself, who can be sent back home to collect them."

"Ours is the only computer like it anywhere," said Boopie. "It's Max's invention, you see." She glanced at the thin man warily, but he said nothing. "Anyway," Boopie went on hastily, "we'd better get you going, Patrick!"

Patrick nodded, his mind racing. There was so much to take in. He knew he should be asking lots more questions, but he didn't really know where to start.

"What if the thing—the Find—what if someone else has already found it, and won't let me have it?" he blurted out.

Boopie shook her head. "That never happens," she said. "People on your side of the Barrier don't take much notice of things from over here. You'll have no trouble on that score, believe me."

"Right, let's get this show on the road," said Max briskly. "Just stand over there, son, and look at the TV for me, will you?" He went over to his computer.

Boopie stood up and he sat down in his chair and began tinkering with the keys.

Patrick did as he was told. The small TV set on the wall sprang into life. The picture was black and white and very fuzzy, and for a moment he couldn't work out what it was. Then he realized that he was watching the TV section of the department store back at Chestnut Tree Village.

"How long have I got?" he asked desperately.

"One week, your time, Patrick," called Boopie. "But, oh, dear, I nearly forgot—wear the same clothes when you come back, will you, sweetie pie? All your episodes will be put together to make one show, eventually."

"Ready?" growled Max. "Right . . . don't look away. . . ."

Patrick held his breath.

"Stop!" shrieked Boopie suddenly, making them both jump. "Oh, heavens, Maxie, I clean forgot to tell him how to get back! Oh, I'm so . . . I just can't think straight these days. . . . Oh, I'm sorry. . . ."

"Make it snappy, Boop, I can't hold the fix!" said Max urgently.

"Same telly set, same time next Saturday, Patrick. And bring your Find with you. Got it?"

Her voice was fading, the room was fading.

"Yes," shouted Patrick. "But. . . ." He tried to turn his head.

"Don't look away!" Max's voice echoed in the dimness.

Patrick felt dizzy and sick. There was a faint ringing in his ears. Boopie's voice. He struggled to hear what she was calling, and finally the words came clear.

"Good Finding, sweetie pie! Good luck!"

"Good-bye," he whispered. And closed his eyes, tight.

8

THE FIRST FINd

Someone trod heavily on Patrick's toe. He opened his eyes. He was back in the department store, and a teenage boy with a startled expression was staring at him. "Sorry," the boy mumbled. "Didn't see you there."

"That's okay," Patrick said vaguely. The boy looked at him in a puzzled way and then shrugged and walked off, past the rows of TV sets and VCRs.

Patrick slowly rubbed his bruised toe against the back of his leg. So he'd made it! And as the thought formed in his mind, he realized that he could still hear the blacksmith striking the anvil on the Chestnut Tree Village clock. About this, at least, Boopie Cupid had been telling the truth. Time had practically stood still.

He began to walk unsteadily toward the exit. His knees were wobbly. He felt in his pocket and pulled out

Clyde O'Brien's clue. With it came a feather—it could only be the feather from Boopie's dress, but he would hardly have recognized it. Instead of being bright, bright yellow, it had faded to a dull creamy color. The writing on the clue-note, too, was very pale. He had to strain his eyes to read it.

Carefully pushing both things back into his pocket, he made his way out of the shop. The clock had finished striking now, and the crowd of people that had surrounded it was breaking up. He could see his mother sitting with her cup of coffee where he had left her. She looked up, saw him, and waved.

Patrick broke into a half jog. He was very glad to see her, looking so familiar and peaceful. He knew he couldn't tell her about "Finders Keepers" and the Barrier and everything, because she'd just think he was imagining things, which he had to admit he often did. She wouldn't believe for a minute that it had all really happened. So he couldn't tell her. But it was awfully good to be back with her all the same.

She smiled as he approached. "Ready to go home, darling?"

He nodded and smiled back. He wanted very much to go home and to get up to his room where he could be alone. He had a lot to think about.

TWO AND a half hours later Patrick sat on his bed with Clyde O'Brien's clue spread out in front of him. No matter which way he looked at it, it still didn't make sense. He strained his eyes to read the faint writing for the hundredth time:

> A tree has died to give me birth,
> But still I shelter feathered friends.
> I'm large and heavy, colored earth,
> With golden fringes my tail ends.
> And where my name and others be,
> My owner's name is plain to see.

It sounded like a sort of animal—a big, heavy animal with a tail that had golden fringes on the end. A lion? Lions were gold-colored. A stuffed lion, maybe? Maybe it was stuffed with feathers, and that's what the second line meant, though it was a strange way of putting it. Still, these riddle-clues were tricky. They did deliberately put things in strange ways, to puzzle you.

A stuffed lion, or some other big animal, with a gold-fringed tail. Yes, that could be it! He crouched over the piece of paper excitedly. He still couldn't see where the dying tree came in, and yet . . . maybe a tree fell on the lion, and that's how it died and got to be stuffed with feathers. . . . No—that sounded funny, even to him. And what about "colored earth"? Where did that fit in? And as for the stuff about the names. . . .

"Patrick! Lunch!" Judith's voice floated up the stairs. "Patrick!"

"Coming!" he yelled. He snatched up the crumpled paper and put it into his desk drawer, beside the feather. How could he possibly find something by next Saturday, when he didn't even know what it was? Why make it so hard? It was ridiculous! What a stupid, idiotic game! It was probably better just to forget all about it. But as he left his room, he felt cautiously for the little beeper-brooch, to make sure it was still firmly attached to his T-shirt where Boopie Cupid had put it. It was just as well to be prepared.

"DAD," SAID Patrick at lunch. "Would there be any stuffed lions around here?"

Paul stared at him for a minute. "Now, there's a question you don't get asked every day," he said finally, turning to Judith.

Claire giggled.

"At the museum there might be one," said Judith helpfully, frowning at Claire.

"Is the museum in our area?" Patrick persisted. "Is it?"

"Well, it's in our general area," said Paul. "But I wouldn't say it was in our actual, immediate area, no. What is this, mate? Something for school?"

"It'll be a project," Claire said knowledgeably, returning to her salad. "We started them in his grade."

"I just have to find out," said Patrick.

"About stuffed animals?" Judith asked carefully. "Or just stuffed lions?"

Patrick felt himself blushing and looked at his plate. "I don't know, really," he said gruffly. He wished he'd never started this conversation.

"I know about lions," Danny piped up, not wanting to be left out.

"Yes, darling. Eat up your cheese, now," Judith said.

There was a short, thoughtful pause.

"They have big teeth, and they go 'grrrrr.'" Danny bared his teeth ferociously.

"Oh, yuck!" squealed Claire. Paul and Patrick covered their eyes.

"Danny, don't growl with your mouth full," said Judith calmly. "It looks disgusting. Claire, be quiet!"

"Could we go to the museum this afternoon?" Patrick asked hopefully. It was worth a try.

His parents looked at one another. "Oh, well, why not?" said Paul.

Patrick's heart beat faster. The treasure hunt had started.

BUT THE museum was a big disappointment. There were plenty of stuffed animals there, but the beeper-brooch didn't make a single sound, no matter how close Patrick went to the cases in which they were kept. He was very quiet on the way home, and didn't even complain about sitting in the middle at the back while Danny chattered endlessly about the dinosaur and whale skeletons, which seemed to be about the only things he'd remembered.

"I like the bird gallery best," Claire said, cutting into Danny's theories as to exactly how the "skelingtons" had lost their skin.

"Yes," agreed Paul. "The birds are great."

"The songs are nice," Judith said. "But, I don't know, it's a bit grim seeing all those little dead birds with fake eyes staring out at you. I'd rather see them alive, wouldn't you? In trees, and alive—instead of dead and stuffed in a wood and glass case."

Patrick lifted his head. Birds in a wood and glass case. Wood came from trees. . . .

A tree has died to give me birth,
But still I shelter feathered friends. . . .

That could be it! But the beeper hadn't sounded at the museum.

"Have you seen that little case of birds in the antique shop window at Chestnut Tree Village, Mum? The hummingbirds?" Claire asked Judith. "They're so sweet! I nearly went in and asked about it for your birthday, but then I thought that seeing they were real birds you might not like it."

"Quite right!" exclaimed Judith. "Yes, I've seen them. Poor little hummingbirds."

"Do any of them have golden tails?" exploded Patrick.

Claire stared at him. "They might have," she said cautiously.

"Mum, Mum, can we go to Chestnut Tree Village now?" begged Patrick.

"Patrick, you and I were there this morning!" said Judith. "And we've just taken you to the museum. You're never satisfied!"

"But—"

"Patrick, there's no way in the world I'm going anywhere but home at this point," said Paul firmly. "I'll take you to see the hummingbirds another day. Okay?"

"Tomorrow? Tomorrow, Dad?"

"We'll see. If there's time."

Patrick slumped back in his seat. He knew what that

meant. And he knew better than to keep nagging now. But he wasn't going to give up. The clues, and the place—Chestnut Tree Village, right near the clock that weakened the Barrier—it all fitted. He knew without a shadow of a doubt that the case of hummingbirds in the antique shop window was Clyde O'Brien's missing object. It all fitted. And if he was going to win that computer, and have a chance of trying for a second Find and even bigger prizes, he just had to get it—one way or another.

9

PROBLEMS

Fortunately for Patrick, Sunday was wet and miserable and Danny was bored and miserable. By midmorning Paul and Judith were only too happy to consider going to Chestnut Tree Village for lunch. Danny's whining had succeeded where any amount of Patrick's nagging would have failed.

As they drove, splashing through puddles, into the car park, it became clear that a lot of other parents had decided to save their sanity by using the Village as a giant playground for an hour or two. The car park seethed with hopeful-looking men and women pushing strollers and leading impatient toddlers toward the delights of McDonald's, the coin-operated rides, and the toy departments of the various stores.

Patrick's family joined the crowd and ambled to the Village entrance. There they hesitated. Up, or down?

"If we go upstairs now," Patrick suggested casually,

"Danny can see the clock strike twelve. It's nearly time."

"Good idea," said Judith briskly. "And of course, my devious darling, you can then go and see the hummingbirds at the shop opposite, can't you?"

Patrick tried not to smile. "I could," he admitted, leading the way to the escalator. "If I wanted to."

The antique shop was directly opposite Smithy's, the coffee shop where Patrick and his mother had stopped the morning before. It was strange to be there again and to remember how depressed he'd been, sitting down at the little table to watch the clock, thinking he'd never find out for sure about "Finders Keepers." He left the others standing quietly with the rest of the crowd waiting for the big twelve o'clock strike and walked toward the antique shop window. He forced himself to move slowly. He didn't want to make them too curious.

His hand felt nervously for the beeper-brooch. Yes, it was still there, pinned to the inside of his T-shirt. Under his hand he could feel his heart beating violently, and suddenly he felt a terrible pang of doubt. He'd really jumped to conclusions about the case of hummingbirds. What if he'd been wrong? When you thought about it, Clyde O'Brien's clue could mean all sorts of things. His feet dragged. He didn't want to find out he'd been wrong.

Now he could see the wooden case of brightly colored birds, right in the center of the antique shop win-

dow. The tiny birds sat on twigs, behind a pane of glass. They looked alive. Their feathers shone like jewels against the dark wood of the little box.

"A tree has died to give me birth. . . ." Yes, the box was made of wood.

"But still I shelter feathered friends. . . ." Yes, the birds were there, all right.

"I'm large and heavy, colored earth. . . ." The box was colored brown—of course—like earth.

He took a breath and stepped forward.

And softly but urgently the little beeper-brooch began to call. He jumped violently, clasped his hand over it, and looked over his shoulder in dismay. Surely everyone would hear.

But he was lucky, for at that moment the Chestnut Tree Village clock began to strike. No one was paying any attention to him or his madly piping little alarm.

He stole forward till his nose was pressed against the glass of the shop window. The shop was dim and empty, and its door was tightly shut. But that didn't disturb him. He hadn't really expected to find it open on a Sunday. He'd have to get back sometime during the week and get the birds. His excitement died down a little. That was going to be tricky. Boopie had told him that there'd be no trouble—that no one from his side would object when one of the missing objects was claimed. Well, that had seemed reasonable when she said it, but it seemed pretty unreasonable now. Why should whoever owned this shop just let him take away something so pretty and valuable looking?

"Aren't they lovely?" Claire loomed up beside him, giving him the shock of his life. He gaped at her and backed away.

"What's up with you?" she demanded. Then she looked around curiously. "Listen to that! Can you hear that alarm?" She put her ear to the shop window. Patrick went on backing away, his hand clamped to his chest in what he hoped was a casual manner.

"Patrick!" she shouted in exasperation. "Come back! Can you hear. . . ? Oh, too late, it's stopped. You missed it, silly."

Patrick breathed again.

WHEN Judith came to tuck him into bed that night, she found him counting the coins and bills in his money tin.

"Hello, moneybags," she said. "Haven't you got a lot?"

Patrick sighed. "I wish I had some more," he said. "Could you give me some jobs for money tomorrow?"

"You don't do most of the jobs you're supposed to do now," Judith pointed out. "Why should I pay you to do other ones?"

"I *do* do my jobs—mostly—often!" protested Patrick. "Please, Mum!"

"Oh, well, I'll see," said Judith. "Pop into bed now. It's late." She looked at him thoughtfully. "Are you okay, darling? You look a bit. . . ."

"I'm fine," said Patrick quickly. "I'm fine, Mum." He got quickly into bed, pulled up the covers, and smiled at her angelically.

She looked at him doubtfully for a moment, then smiled back and bent to kiss him.

"Tell you what," she said, brushing the hair back from his forehead. "If you can find Danny's boot, which has been missing for at least a fortnight somewhere in this dump of a house, I'll pay you a reward! How about that?"

"I'll try," he said. But he didn't have much hope. They'd already looked everywhere for that yellow boot, and he had a feeling that, like single socks, single yellow boots weren't nearly important enough to waste the energy of a lazy Barrier Guard. He doubted they'd ever see that particular missing object again!

After Judith had turned off the light and tiptoed away, he lay staring into the darkness. He had to get some more money together—that was the first problem—but Dad would probably lend him some, if he asked for it in the right way.

The second problem wasn't so easily solved. He had to go back to Chestnut Tree Village and get the birds. And he had to return again on Saturday morning, because he had to use the same television set as before to get back to "Finders Keepers." Boopie had called that out last thing—obviously it was important. He tossed his head on the pillow. Sometimes it was rotten being a kid. You were so helpless! You had to depend on other people to take you places; you weren't allowed to go anywhere on your own. Mum probably wouldn't want to go back to the Village after school this week—or next Saturday, if it came to that. She'd been twice this weekend. Dad certainly wouldn't.

Claire? She was a possibility, if Mum would let her take him alone, which she never had up to now. Who then? Someone nice. Someone who'd be kind to a poor little boy and take him where he wanted to go without asking too many questions. Someone who wasn't too busy to help him. Someone who liked him. Someone who could be talked into things.

And at that, Patrick smiled to himself in the dark, because he'd thought of the perfect person.

"WELL, of course I'll take you, Patrick. I'd be happy to," said Estelle when Patrick asked her the following afternoon. "If your mum doesn't have any objections, of course, dear heart," she added hastily.

"Oh, she won't mind, Estelle, of course she won't," Patrick urged. "When can we go?"

Estelle's soft, timid face grew thoughtful. "Well—ah—today we can't go, of course, because today I'm here, aren't I? And tomorrow . . . now what do I do tomorrow? Oh, yes, on Tuesdays I go to Simpson's, for the ironing. Wednesday. . . ."

"Wednesday you come here again," said Patrick.

She smiled at him vaguely. "Yes. And Thursdays I take my next-door neighbor's dog walkies, in the afternoon."

"Could you miss out this Thursday?" Patrick asked hopefully. This wasn't sounding too promising. He'd had no idea Estelle had such a packed program.

"Oh, I really couldn't do that, dear heart," said Estelle gently. "Porky needs his walk, living in an apartment, you know. He goes all funny if he doesn't get out every day."

"What about Friday, then?" Patrick tried desperately.

Estelle paused. Her brow wrinkled in concentration. "Oh, Patrick," she said at last, "I'm so sorry. I can't do it on Friday, either. I clean at the Vernons' then."

Patrick stared at her helplessly. He couldn't believe his bad luck. He was so close to his prize, and he just couldn't take the final few steps.

She shook her head sadly, her wispy hair floating away from her face in fine strands. Then she brightened. "But Saturday morning would be all right," she said. "As early as you like. Saturday morning I always go to Chestnut Tree Village anyway. It's my little outing."

"Saturday. . . ." Patrick thought about it. Well, he had to get to Chestnut Tree Village on Saturday morning as well, to get back to "Finders Keepers." And if the worst came to the worst, he could go in and buy the hummingbirds from the antique shop just before he left, instead of earlier in the week as he'd planned. It was cutting it pretty fine, but still—it might be the only way.

"Thanks, Estelle," he said at last. "Saturday morning would be terrific."

She nodded, looking pleased.

"You won't forget, will you?" said Patrick anxiously.

"Oh, no," she said. "I'll write it down in my little book. That's what I do, you see, because—well, you know, my memory's not the best. I'll write it down now, dear heart, and then you can be sure in your mind." From her handbag she pulled out a little red notebook. She turned the pages.

"Now, I'll write you down for Saturday, Patrick, at . . . what time, dear heart?"

"Could you pick me up here at eight-thirty?"

She nodded and wrote. Patrick looked at her with gratitude. She was so nice, Estelle. And so gentle and sort of lonely. Not like other grown-ups he knew at all. Somehow you felt like looking after her, instead of thinking it should be the other way around. He watched her white fingers writing. The nails were cut short, and she only wore one uninteresting-looking ring—no watch, even. She didn't seem to have many different clothes, or jewelry, or anything like that. She'd always looked the same, though she'd been coming two after-noons a week for about three months now. And she was so pale and quiet. He wondered why.

Later, when Judith and Paul were home, and Danny was tucked away in bed, he asked them.

"Well. . . ." They looked at each other, as if they were deciding what to say.

"She probably hasn't got enough money for nice clothes," said Claire knowingly. "Maybe not even enough to eat properly. She wouldn't earn much from walking people's dogs and minding kids and things. She should get a proper job."

"Claire, how would you know?" demanded Judith. "Don't be so free with your opinions about other people, please. It's Estelle's business how she runs her life, not yours!"

"Yeah!" said Patrick, and he looked scornfully at Claire, who flushed and tossed her head. But in bed that night he thought about what she'd said and decided that he'd do something really nice for Estelle when this "Finders Keepers" business was over. He thought for a few minutes about what he could do for Estelle, to make her happy. But soon his mind drifted away—to Lucky Lance Lamont, and Boopie Cupid, and how the audience would clap and cheer next Saturday when he turned up with Clyde O'Brien's treasure and claimed his prize. Sighing with satisfaction, he turned over and fell happily asleep.

As THE week went by and it became clear to Patrick that he wasn't going to get to Chestnut Tree Village any afternoon after school, his happiness and satisfaction began to ebb away. By Wednesday he was thoughtful. By Thursday he was worried. By Friday he was panic-stricken. What if something happened tomorrow morning to stop him getting the case of hummingbirds? What if the shop was too crowded, and he couldn't get served by ten o'clock? What if the shop was closed? What if

. . . what if the case of birds had been sold? He stared unseeingly at the TV screen and bit his knuckles fiercely.

"Why are you biting your own hand, Patrick?" asked Danny curiously from his perch on the couch. He put his own chubby paw into his mouth and chewed at it experimentally. "Ow, it hurts! Patrick? It hurts!"

"Well, don't do it, then," said Patrick irritably. "And don't talk. I'm watching."

Danny stared silently at him for a moment, then slipped off the couch. When Patrick looked again, he'd gone.

10

Feathered Friends

On Saturday morning Patrick was up and dressed by seven o'clock. He put on the same T-shirt he'd worn last week, with the beeper-brooch carefully pinned inside it, and the same jeans, with all the money he'd been able to scrape together in the pocket. He even brushed his hair. He had breakfast while everyone else was still in bed. He tried to watch TV. By eight o'clock he was prowling the hallway, waiting for Estelle, looking at his watch every few minutes. Then he remembered his watch ran a few minutes fast and went back to the kitchen to irritate the rest of the family by switching the radio dial around till he heard the time and could make it exactly right.

"Patrick, for heaven's sake, sit down!" Paul ordered at last. "Let us have our breakfast in peace, will you? What's wrong with you? You're acting weird."

"He's been acting weird all week," Claire announced with her mouth full. They all looked at him.

By this time Patrick was feeling so anxious and jumpy that he could hardly speak. He widened his eyes and tried to smile unweirdly. It didn't help. They went on staring at him, and now they all looked quite startled. He wondered what he looked like. Judith opened her mouth to speak.

He was saved by the doorbell. "Estelle!" he managed to gasp, and ran for it. At last, at last, this terrible week of waiting was over. He was on his way.

IT TOOK much longer to get to Chestnut Tree Village by bus. In the car you were there in ten or twelve minutes, but the bus crawled around all sorts of side streets, continually stopping to pick people up or let them off. The blacksmith was striking his anvil to mark nine-thirty by the time Patrick and Estelle arrived beside the clock. Patrick looked frantically over to the antique shop on the other side of the plaza. Its door stood open, and lights shone inside. It was open!

"Could you wait for me, Estelle, while I just go over there?" asked Patrick, pointing to the shop.

"Shouldn't I go with you, dear heart?" said Estelle anxiously. "I don't want you to get lost." She was being particularly slow and fluttering this morning, of all mornings. She'd wanted to go home and check that her door was properly locked, because she'd left her ring in the bathroom and thought a burglar would walk in and steal it. Then she thought she'd left the iron on. Then she found a hole in her stocking. It was all Patrick could do to get her to the bus stop. By the time she'd left her purse on the bus and had to jump back on to get it, he was a nervous wreck.

"I won't get lost. I'll come straight back," said Patrick, in a fever of impatience. He felt for the money in his pocket. Yes, it was there, safe and sound. "You just wait here, Estelle." Suddenly, he had a brain wave. "I know! You have a cup of coffee, at Smithy's, over there, and I'll meet you there. That's what Mum always does."

She looked at him doubtfully. "Oh. Well, I suppose that's all right, dear heart. If that's what your mother does. And I would like a cup of coffee. That would be lovely." She looked around. "I really love this place, you know," she said. "Especially up here, near the clock. It's so . . . full of *life*, don't you think so, Patrick?"

He guided her to a seat and saw her safely settled with a waitress taking her order. That had been a good idea, he thought to himself, waving to her as he set off toward the antique shop. Now she was out of the way for as long as it took to drink a cup of coffee, however long that was. Ten minutes at least, he thought. More, if the coffee was very hot. He hoped it would be.

As he approached the shop, he saw that the case of birds was still standing in the window. Thank goodness—it hadn't been sold. He glanced at his watch. Twenty to ten. He still had twenty minutes to buy the birds, get back to Estelle, and then make another excuse to go and look at the TV sets. Plenty of time, really. But his heart was beating hard as he walked, and when the beeper-brooch began to sound, it beat even harder. He covered the spot where it was pinned with his hand to muffle the sound, but you could still hear it quite plainly. Well, it couldn't be helped. He'd just have to explain it away somehow.

He hesitated a moment at the shop door, suddenly overtaken by a flood of shyness. He'd never actually bought anything more important than an ice cream or a carton of milk before. But another glance at his watch propelled him across the threshold and onto the soft carpet inside. This was no time to hold back.

A thin-faced young man was stacking things into a carton at the back of the tiny shop. "Yes, can I help you?" he said, smiling, then he looked at Patrick curiously. "Do you know the alarm on your watch is ringing?"

Patrick felt himself blushing and looked down at his feet. "Um—yeah," he mumbled. "Um—I wanted to buy—that." He pointed to the case of hummingbirds in the window and began fumbling in his pocket for his money.

The young man's eyebrows rose, and his forehead wrinkled with concern. "Oh, I'm sorry," he said, coming forward. "The birds aren't for sale. They belong to the owner. They're just for decoration—to make the window pretty, you know?"

Patrick gulped with horror. "I've got money," he said, pulling his coins, carefully wrapped in the few bills he had, from his pocket.

The man's forehead wrinkled even more. "I really am sorry, but the birds aren't for sale. And, look, even if they were," he went on gently, "they'd cost an awful lot more than you've got there."

Patrick stared at him, aghast. The beeper-brooch piping away on his chest seemed to be urging him to do something—quickly. But what could he do? It wasn't fair. Boopie had said he'd be able to get the missing objects easily, once he had found them. She had said no one on this side would really care about them.

"Could I borrow the birds, then?" he burst out, in desperation.

The man shook his head. "I'm very sorry to disappoint you, but they're very valuable. I couldn't let them out of the shop. I really couldn't."

"That's okay." Defeated, Patrick turned to go. The man went back to his stacking, watching him out of the corner of his eye. "You're rather keen on birds, are you?" he said sympathetically. Patrick shrugged, biting at his lip to stop it trembling, and moved to the door. The young man came after him and put a hand on his shoulder.

"Never mind," he said, raising his voice over the sound of the beeper-brooch. It had suddenly begun peeping more loudly than ever. It must know, Patrick thought, that he was giving up. It was urging him to try harder. But there was nothing he could do.

"Take this," the man said, pushing a dusty old book into his hands. "A little present, eh? No charge. You may as well have it as the church sale, isn't that right? Why not?"

"Thank you," Patrick muttered, and tried to smile. The man was being kind because he was sorry for him. It wasn't his fault that Patrick couldn't get the birds.

He stumbled from the shop with the bulky book under his arm, stuffing his useless money back into his pocket. The beeper-brooch was going crazy, and now that he was outside, people had started looking at him. He ducked his head and scuttled toward the clock, trying to escape their curious eyes. It wasn't until he had actually reached the clock and was skulking behind it, getting ready to face Estelle, that he realized something was wrong.

He had left the shop and the hummingbirds far behind. But the beeper-brooch was still sounding. It should have gone quiet long ago. Was it broken? Maybe it had blown a fuse or something when it realized he wasn't going to get what it was tracking. Anyway, it sounded as though it was about to blow a fuse now. *Peep-peep-peep-peep-peep*—it was enough to drive anyone mad. "Shut up, will you?" he hissed at it, giving it a little punch. "I can't do anything about it!"

But the beeper-brooch kept it up. He was getting desperate. He unpinned it and stuffed it into his pocket, but the noise went on. "Stupid thing!" he raged at it.

"Stop it! Everyone's looking. Stop it or I'll smash you up!"

He knew he was being childish, but he couldn't help it. He'd so wanted to win at this. He'd worked and planned so carefully, and now it had all gone to waste. In a rage, he pulled the little brooch from his pocket and looked at it through angry tears. "I'll stomp on you!" he threatened. The book that the antique shop man had given him slipped from under his arm and hit the ground with a dusty thud, falling open on the tiles. He bent, furiously, to pick it up, and saw that it was filled with strange, light-colored pictures of birds. It had fallen open at a page marked with a wide ribbon bookmark, finished with a dull gold fringe.

He stared at it. The beeper-brooch peeped wildly. And then he understood.

"A tree has died to give me birth. . . ." Paper came from trees. Books came from trees.

"But still I shelter feathered friends. . . ." The book was filled with pictures of birds.

"I'm large and heavy"—it was—"colored earth. . . ." The cover was dusty brown.

"With golden fringes my tail ends. . . ." The bookmark.

"And where my name and others be. . . ." He crouched down quickly and turned to the front of the book. There were the names—the title of the book, *Birds of the World*, and the author's and illustrator's names, and. . . .

"My owner's name is plain to see." There, faintly, in spidery handwriting, was the name of the book's owner. Clyde O'Brien.

Trembling, Patrick picked up the book and clasped the singing beeper-brooch firmly in his other hand. He looked at his watch. A minute to ten. He still had time. He ran toward the entrance to the department store where the TV sets were. No time now to explain to Estelle.

She saw him as he ran and half rose to her feet. "Back in a minute, Estelle," he roared, ignoring her startled cry and charging on. He swung into the store, panting.

He reached the TV set he'd used before and switched to Channel 8. He heard the clock begin to strike. He saw Lucky Lamont's face appear on the screen.

"Has our Finder been successful?" Lucky was shouting. "We'll find out, right now. Patrick, are you ready to go on playing 'Finders Keepers'?"

"*Yes!*" Patrick shouted joyously, and closed his eyes.

11

Boopie Helps Out

The audience was clapping and shouting, Lucky was pounding him on the back, rollicking music was playing. Patrick blinked, dazed, at the bright lights.

Lucky took the book from his hands and held it high above his head. "Clyde O'Brien!" he shouted dramatically. "Is this your missing object?"

Clyde O'Brien stumbled from his place and, escorted by a beaming Boopie Cupid, half ran to Lucky's side. He didn't have to answer the question. The relief on his grim face was answer enough. He held out his hand for the book and Lucky gave it to him. Eagerly he thumbed through the pages.

Patrick stared at the book. It didn't look faded and shabby anymore. Now the cover was rich, leathery brown, and the pictures were bright, glowing with life. Even the ribbon bookmark was shining like silk, its golden fringe catching the light. But Clyde O'Brien wasn't stopping to look at the pictures or admire the bookmark. He was looking for something. And about three-quarters of the way through, he found it.

He pulled a folded, yellowing piece of paper from the book and opened it with strong, blunt fingers that trembled with excitement.

"Eureka?" bawled Lucky.

Unable to speak, Clyde O'Brien nodded. He dropped the book to the floor, pulled out his wallet, and carefully put the paper inside it. Then he suddenly turned and bolted away, without another word.

"Well, now, folks, there's one very happy man," cried Lucky, looking after him in some confusion. "He's so happy he forgot to say good-bye. Or thank you to his Finder. So we'll do it for him, will we, folks?" He and Boopie clapped, and the audience joined in enthusiastically, but Patrick stood looking after the man who had left, then slowly picked up the book. It was too beautiful just to lie there underfoot, and it reminded him of the old books his father treasured at home.

"Now, Pat, time to spin that wheel," cried Lucky. "Let's see what you can win!"

Boopie Cupid took Patrick's arm and led him to the glittering wheel.

"Look at all those prizes, Pat," drooled Lucky. "I'll bet there's something there you'd really like, eh?"

"The computer," said Patrick loudly. He had practiced this. He had thought about this moment so often in the last week. "The Ezy-way computer and the games."

"Well, we'll see if you're in luck!" smiled Lucky happily. "Spin that wheel, Pat!"

Patrick stared at him dumbly. He'd thought he'd get to choose his prize! He'd thought. . . .

"Give it all you've got, Pat!" urged Lucky.

Patrick took a deep breath and spun the wheel as hard as he could. It whirled around with enormous speed. He crossed his fingers and hoped with all his might, holding the picture of that computer in his mind, as if by doing that he might make the wheel stop in the right place.

It was slowing down. It was stopping. It had stopped.

"Number nineteen, number nineteen!" shouted Lucky. "Boopie, tell us what Patrick has won!"

Boopie looked up from a list in her hand. Her cheeks were flushed. "Patrick has won this *adorable* music box, Lucky." She threw out her arm, shedding a few more feathers as she did so. The makeup girl in the pink smock rushed from the sidelines and put something small and brightly colored in her hand. Boopie teetered over to Patrick, smiling rather stiffly.

"Hey, isn't that cute!" crooned Lucky admiringly. "What a great prize! The Toytown Musical Merry-Go-Round, from our friends at the House of Bonning, makers of fine china and bathroom products."

Boopie wound the music box. The little horses went

around, and a chiming tune played. The audience sighed with pleasure. Patrick couldn't remember ever having been so disappointed before in his whole life. He blinked hard and tried to smile.

"Well, this is exciting," said Lucky hastily. "Now, Patrick, you've got the big decision to make. Will you risk this fabulous prize and go on to try for a second Find? It's up to you. You can go away now, and take home your musical merry-go-round with no strings attached, yours to keep. Or you can stay on, to try for more great prizes. What do you say?"

"I don't know," muttered Patrick, eyeing the tinkling merry-go-round. A week's misery and trouble, just for that! He didn't know if he could go through it all again

for such an uncertain result. He might win something even more useless next time.

"Great idea! Leave it to Boopie Cupid!" cried Lucky. Patrick looked up and saw Boopie just stepping back after whispering in Lucky's ear.

"Boopie thinks we can make Pat's choice a little bit harder, folks!" Lucky said, twinkling at the audience. He turned to Patrick. "I know it must be hard to think about risking your prize, Pat. But we want to tempt you. You want that computer, right?"

Patrick nodded dumbly.

"Okay," said Lucky, pointing a finger at him playfully. "How about if we say to you that if you come back with Find number two, and guarantee to go on to Find number three, we *give* you that computer as a bonus prize. Now, what do you say to that? Will you leave us, or go on?"

"I'll go on!" yelped Patrick, and beamed at Boopie Cupid.

The audience went wild, and Lucky announced a commercial break.

Boopie had her nose powdered by the girl in pink and then trotted over to where Patrick stood.

"Thanks for suggesting about the computer," said Patrick awkwardly.

"Oh, sweetie pie, I nearly died when I saw what you'd won!" whispered Boopie in a shocked voice. "It was the least I could do. Really, they have a nerve on this show sometimes. And as for that Mr. O'Brien!

Well! We've never had a ruder Seeker on the show, ever. I mean, he didn't even thank you, or us, or anything! Some people!" She sighed. Under her makeup she looked tired and strained.

"What was that paper he got out of the book?" asked Patrick curiously. "A treasure map, or something?"

Boopie sniffed. "Oh, nothing as interesting as that. It was a will—a moldy old will. His grandpa died, you see, and left him all his money. Well, that's what Clyde said his grandpa had promised him, anyway. The rest of the family didn't believe it. No wonder, because you couldn't say Mr. O'Brien was very likable, or charming or anything, could you? So he had to find his grandpa's will, to prove it. Anyway, old Grandpa O'Brien, whose name was Clyde, too, was a great bird-watcher, or something, and that book was his most precious possession. Everyone thought his will would be in the bank, but it turned out it wasn't. They looked everywhere. Then they finally thought of asking his doctor, who was about the only person who'd been near the poor old chap for months, and he said the old man had shown him the will, tucked into his favorite book, in his study." She made a face.

"That was when Clyde O'Brien realized he'd made a big mistake. He'd cleaned out all his grandpa's 'rubbish,' as he so charmingly put it, so he could move into the house himself. He'd sold all the books—including the old man's favorite, *Birds of the World*, to a secondhand shop down beside the Barrier. So he was in the biggest

panic by the time he wrote to us. Because the shop-
keeper said he hadn't sold the book, but it had gone.
Right after a truck ran into the Barrier and split it, just
opposite his shop. He knew where the book, and the
will—and his hopes of all his grandpa's money—had
gone. Over to your side."

"What a pig!" exclaimed Patrick indignantly. "He
didn't care about his grandfather's lovely book at all. Or
about his grandfather, either. He just cared about the
money."

Boopie shrugged. "It takes all kinds to make a world,
I guess," she said. But Patrick was angry.

"Why would you choose someone like that to be on
'Finders Keepers,' anyway?" he demanded.

Boopie shrugged again. "Well, I don't choose the
Seekers, sweetie pie," she said. "Don't blame me. The
producer chooses them, with Max. They pick people
whose things Max can get a fix on, and who've got interesting stories. The audience likes to know the Seekers
are really desperate. We always tell the Seekers' stories
before the Finder comes. That makes it more exciting,
you see. Just like you, the Seekers only get to play in
one game, you know. If you don't find their missing
object, they don't get another chance."

"I didn't realize that," said Patrick slowly. "You
mean, for all three of them, this is the only game?"

She nodded seriously. "That's why they all look so
nervous, you see, and why Eleanor Doon and Wendy
Minelli were as glad as horrible old Clyde to see you

come back with the Find and decide to go on playing. If you'd failed, or chosen not to go on, they'd have lost their chance to have *their* things found. And they care. They care a lot." She sighed and her painted lips tilted into a rather sad little smile. "It's no fun being a Seeker," she said.

Patrick looked at her doubtfully. It was bad enough when he'd been trying to win just for himself. But now he had to worry about the Seekers as well!

"Anyway, cheer up, sugarplum," said Boopie, smoothing her feathers. "The ad break's nearly over, and you've got to choose another Seeker. I wonder which one you'll get this time!"

12
THE BARRIER

"Which Seeker will our Finder choose this time?" boomed Lucky Lamont. "Wendy Minelli? Or Eleanor Doon?" He grinned feverishly at the two Seekers left behind the desk. They looked anxiously back.

Boopie held up the silver basket. The drumroll began. "You're chosen by chance and you take your chance in 'Finders Keepers,'" crowed Lucky. Patrick took a folded slip of paper between his fingers. He gave it to Lucky, who looked inside and beamed at Wendy Minelli. She went pink with excitement and leaned forward in her chair.

"Sorry, Wendy, you'll have to wait a little longer!" Lucky laughed, wagging his finger at her. The audience laughed with him, and Wendy Minelli sank back, baffled and embarrassed. Patrick looked at Lucky disgustedly. What a mean trick to play, just to get a laugh.

"Eleanor, you're the lucky one," Lucky cried. "Boopie, will you read Eleanor's clue again?"

Boopie took the paper and read in a careful, high voice:

> "My first is in fur but not in fun,
> My second means just me alone,
> My third is third as well in run,
> My fourth begins my saddest groan.
> I have three hearts of deepest red,
> In shining gold they make their bed."

She handed the clue to Patrick, who bit his lip and pushed the paper into his pocket. The rhyme still made no sense at all to him.

"Not so hard, Pat, eh?" teased Lucky. "All right then, off you go. Boopie, take him away! Good Finding, Pat!"

"Good Finding!" roared the audience.

Again Patrick let Boopie take his arm and lead him away. Wendy Minelli gave him a little wave as he passed, but Eleanor Doon leaned over and grasped his arm with a cold, damp hand. The knobbly rings that clustered thickly on her fingers bit uncomfortably into his skin. "Good Finding!" she murmured through tight lips. "Don't fail me, will you?" Patrick met her dull gray eyes and couldn't look away.

"Come on, Finder," trilled Boopie Cupid, pulling him away from the long, clutching fingers. She hurried him to the studio door and into the corridor.

"Gosh, she's a bit of a horror, isn't she!" she exploded, and giggled. She kicked off her shoes and began to trot down the corridor. "Come on, lovesy!" she called, beckoning to Patrick. "We're behind time. Got to hurry."

But before they got to Max's door, it flew open and Max himself appeared, pulling at his tufty hair and dancing around in frustration. Through the open door came the sound of a computer having hysterics. Beeping, pinging, whistling, and clattering, Max's Ezy-way Plus 3 was making its opinion of things in general very clear.

"I'll have to shut down," shouted Max above the noise. "Don't know what's the matter with the stupid thing now."

"Oh, no, Max," cried Boopie. "Not again. Oh, I can't bear it!"

"Can't be helped," grunted Max. He rushed back into the room, and suddenly the noise stopped dead, leaving an eerie silence in the corridor. Max reappeared, shaking his head. "Done," he said briefly.

"How long will it take to fix, Maxie? How long?" Boopie asked anxiously.

He threw up his hands. "How would I know?" he said grumpily. "An hour? Two?"

Boopie looked worried. "Max, this won't . . . hold things up for us, will it? Time's going by so fast." She glanced quickly at Patrick and lowered her voice. "The TBE, Max. Every hour's precious now. We'll still be able to—you know—later, won't we?"

Patrick jumped and looked at Max anxiously. This sounded ominous. He didn't want to be stuck here for good!

"Boopie, shut up!" snapped Max. "What are you thinking about? Your Finder can hear you, and you're scaring him to death." He turned to Patrick. "Don't fret, son. You'll be all right."

Boopie looked guilty and rattled. "Oh, of course you

will, Patrick. Anyway. I'd better get back to the studio and explain to everyone," she gabbled. "I hope Lucky won't blow a fuse. He's so *hopeless* in a crisis, and he's got a couple of screws loose as it is, in my opinion." She patted Patrick's arm and took the heavy book from him. "Look, sweetie pie," she said. "I'll take you to the cafeteria. You can have something to eat while you're waiting."

"Ask them where my tea is while you're at it, will you?" grunted Max. "It's late, and I'm parched."

Boopie ushered Patrick out of the room and trotted off down the corridor. She was obviously worried and upset. Patrick followed her nervously.

"It will be all right, won't it?" he ventured.

"What? Oh, oh, yes, sweetie pie, don't worry," murmured Boopie in an absentminded way. But as though his words had spurred her on, she began to walk faster. Patrick jogged along beside her, his heart beating hard in his chest. He didn't like this. Not one little bit. And what was this TBE?

IN THE cafeteria Patrick stared into space, wishing he had someone to talk to. The bored-looking girl behind the counter didn't seem to notice he was there. Several people came in—some he recognized from "Finders Keepers," and others were obviously from other parts of the TV studio. There were a couple of clowns in full makeup and a man in a mouse suit at one table. At the table next to his, two men in overalls were eating meat pies and talking loudly about a black and oily piece of equipment they'd brought with them in a plastic bag. No one paid any attention to him at all.

"Anyhow, it'll take a week to fix at least, I reckon," growled one of the men in overalls, kicking at the plastic bag at his feet. "They'll just have to wait."

"There's something going on round here that we don't know about, if you ask me," said the other man. "Why's everything breaking down all of a sudden? It isn't normal."

The first man took a huge bite of his pie and chewed thoughtfully. "It's been going on for months, in fact," he said with his mouth full, and then frowned. "Even the pies have gone bad. This thing's dry as old Harry. That woman who used to be here made beauties. That pretty blond woman. What happened to her?"

"On leave," said the other sourly. "All right for some. We've got no chance of getting any time off for the rest of the year, the way things are going. And you know what I reckon? I reckon it's that computer—the 'Finders Keepers' computer—that's at the root of it all. Think of the power it takes out of the system. And I've heard it's been playing up."

Patrick pricked up his ears.

The first man nodded slowly. "You could be on to something there, mate," he agreed. "When you think about it, that computer isn't natural, is it? I always said that. It isn't natural, bringing Finders through the Barrier. They belong on their side, like we belong on ours, and they should stay there. Were you here when the first lot came over?"

His friend shook his head.

"Well, I was," said the man, "and I can tell you there were some goings-on then that'd make your hair curl." He bent over the table and lowered his voice. Patrick strained to catch what he was saying.

"It's very hush-hush," murmured the man. "So don't repeat it. But, see, in those days they didn't know about TBE. . . ."

Patrick almost jumped out of his chair. TBE again. What was TBE?

". . . Trans Barrier Effect," the man was continuing. "You know, the thing Finders get if they stay on this side too long?"

"Yeah, I've heard about it," said the other man. "Lose their memories or something, don't they?"

"And the rest!" whispered his friend. "Stay here too long and they're history, mate. Just get more and more faded . . . no memory . . . no color. . . ." He paused. Patrick clutched the edge of the table. "In the end," the man muttered, "they just fade away to nothing—disappear, mate. That's what happens to them, poor chumps."

The first man dropped the last of his pie onto his plate, uneaten. He looked sick.

Patrick leaned back in his chair, horrified. No wonder Boopie Cupid was so worried about staying on time, avoiding delays. No wonder she was frightened and worried when the computer broke down. When they were in the computer room, she'd nearly told him about the danger he was in. But Max had stopped her.

Patrick felt very small and alone. They weren't being honest with him. They wanted him to go on with the game, whatever the danger. That was why Boopie had suggested the computer as an extra prize. She'd thought he might drop out. He'd thought she really cared about him, but she was just trying to make sure he'd go on playing. And her plan had worked!

Well, now at least he knew the score. They'd bribed him with the computer. They thought they had him now. Well, maybe they did and maybe they didn't. He'd decide for himself. If he did go on, it'd be because he wanted to, understanding all the risks, not because they were fooling him.

Patrick squared his shoulders. He was angry, and somehow he didn't feel so scared anymore. He looked up just in time to see Wendy Minelli walk through the door. She waved at him and came over to his table.

"I suppose I shouldn't be talking to you, really," she said. "But it can't hurt as long as we don't talk about— about my clue or anything, can it?"

Patrick shrugged. He wasn't going to worry about their rules anymore. He didn't owe them anything.

"To tell you the truth," said Wendy, pulling out a chair, "I was awfully glad when they said I could get out of the studio for a while. That Eleanor Doon woman isn't very talkative. And apparently we've got ages to wait. There's something wrong with the computer, they said. Is that what you heard?"

"Yeah," said Patrick gloomily. "They're fixing it now. I hope they hurry up."

She hesitated a moment, then put out her hand and patted his arm. "You're pretty young to be doing this, aren't you?" she murmured. "It must be hard."

He looked at her gratefully. Her freckled face was friendly, and her rough-skinned hand warm. "It is hard," he began, "especially because, you know, I don't really understand—all this. All about the Barrier, and everything. If it's really true." He looked at her sideways.

She laughed. "Oh, it's true, all right. Only too true. In fact, you just come with me and I'll show you. Come on—it'll only take ten minutes!"

She hustled Patrick over to the door and led him down a passage. "I just can't understand why you haven't caught on to it, over on your side," she said. "I mean, you lose so many things through Barrier breaks. The Guards throw them back, of course—well, most of the time—but still. . . ." She pushed open a little door marked EXIT and led Patrick into the open air. He blinked in the sunlight and looked around curiously.

Outside the high wire fence that surrounded the TV station there was a grass strip and a road that climbed up a small hill. Perfectly normal-looking houses lined the road. Everything looked perfectly ordinary—so ordinary that Patrick was suddenly overwhelmed by the suspicion that after all this must be just a complicated joke, like "Candid Camera," and that all this talk about Barriers and neighboring time streams was just to see how far he could be fooled. Maybe TV cameras were filming him right now. He glanced over his shoulder nervously.

"Just up the hill and round behind those trees, Patrick," said Wendy, leading the way energetically. As she walked, she went on talking. "Surely people notice how often things get lost, over on your side?" she said. "And even if they don't, you'd think they *would* take notice when something just disappears and the next minute comes back again! I mean, surely once that had happened to you, you'd start to wonder?"

Patrick wrinkled his forehead. "Well, I don't know," he panted, struggling to keep up with her. "At home . . . it doesn't seem like that. I mean, if someone loses something, or can't see it, and then it turns up, they just think they've made a mistake, or not looked properly, or something. They say things like 'It wasn't there a minute ago,' but they don't really mean it. They're just joking. And, you know, I've been thinking, at home it doesn't just happen outside, you know. It happens inside, too. In kitchens and bedrooms, and places like that."

"My old dad reckons the Barrier must be all broken up and jagged on your side, instead of being smooth and flat like it is on ours," Wendy said. "You can tell from the things that come through, he says, that it's in among everything over there. Maybe he's right. It stands to reason that it must be different on your side, or your people would have noticed it. I mean—look at that! You couldn't miss *that*, could you? At least when the sun's shining." She pointed.

The Barrier rose before them, higher than the eye could see, shimmering in the sun, like heat waves rising from a hot road. It had no color. It was just a glimmer in the air. But you couldn't see through it, and it stretched both ways to the horizon. Dotted along its length were little red houses, like tall dog kennels, and groups of tables and stalls, like the cake stalls people set up sometimes on the footpaths outside Chestnut Tree Village.

"What are they?" asked Patrick, fascinated, pointing at the red houses.

"Oh, well, they're the Barrier Guard sentry boxes, Patrick," said Wendy. "See? There's a Guard walking along back to hers now. She's been inspecting her section of the Barrier. Now she's going to have a rest."

Sure enough, a woman in a smart red uniform with brass buttons and a matching cap was marching briskly along the Barrier toward one of the sentry boxes.

"Nice uniform, isn't it?" said Wendy, and sighed. "I used to be a Barrier Guard, you know," she added unexpectedly.

Patrick turned to her, amazed. "*Were* you?" he exclaimed, sounding far more surprised than he had meant.

She smiled at him and ran her hand through her red curls, but her eyes were rather sad. "You can't imagine it, I suppose. Well, it's true. I was a good one, too, if I do say so myself. That was my sentry box—the one that Guard's got now. I had it done up really nicely inside—pictures and flowers and everything. Oh, well." She sighed again.

"What happened?" Patrick blurted out, and then he realized he was being rude and bit his lip. "Oh, sorry," he said. "You don't—I mean, don't tell me if you don't want to."

"Oh, I don't mind," said Wendy Minelli. "But I think it'd be best if I didn't talk about it really. Not yet. Not—" Suddenly she stopped. Her eyes were fixed on the tall figure of the Guard down by the Barrier. She grabbed Patrick's arm. "Look at that!" she cried excitedly. "Now, there you are, Patrick. Look!"

Patrick stared at the Guard, who had stopped and seemed to be shouting into a radio with a long aerial. She kept looking anxiously over her shoulder.

"Look at the Barrier!" hissed Wendy, jiggling his arm and pointing.

Patrick looked. Behind the Guard a black crack had appeared on the shining surface of the Barrier. As he watched, it began to widen and creep toward the ground. The Barrier Guard glanced at it again and shrieked into her radio, shaking her fist. Other red-coated Guards began to run from their own sentry boxes up and down the lines toward her.

"It's quite a big one!" breathed Wendy in Patrick's ear. "Quite a big one. I hope they can handle it."

13
Lost and Found

The crack was widening. The Guards were shouting at each other as they ran toward it, and the people from the little stalls dotted between the sentry boxes had abandoned their tables and were also hurrying to the spot. They were a rather strange-looking group, dressed in a weird array of tattered clothing in all sizes and colors.

"Let's go closer," urged Patrick, tugging at Wendy's arm.

"Oh, we really shouldn't," she murmured uneasily. "You aren't supposed to." Then she shook her head. "Oh, why not!" she said. "What harm can it do? Come on!"

They ran down the hill toward the Barrier. As they drew closer, they could hear the Guards shouting to one another. A tall woman with gold stripes on the arm of her jacket was blowing a whistle and trying to get them organized.

"Listen to them," said Wendy scornfully. "Panicking. That's what happens when you put inexperienced people in charge of weak spots. The Barrier's always breaking round here. They should have their best Guards on duty."

"Were you one of their best people?" asked Patrick.

She looked confused. "Well, put it this way, I've been . . . I had been, I should say, a Guard ever since I left school. It was all I ever wanted to be. Fifteen years I'd worked on the Barrier when—when I made the mistake that cost me my job. Fifteen years! At least I knew what was what. And I didn't panic, no matter what happened."

"So—" Patrick began, but she caught his arm.

"Watch," she said. "It's starting."

A glint of silver shone through the crack in the Barrier. The crack widened. With a rush and a clatter two forks and a dog's bowl shot through the crack and fell to the ground onto a Guard's foot. He kicked out angrily. Another Guard picked up the bowl and began trying to shove it back where it had come from.

"Too rough," said Wendy Minelli, shaking her head.

Sure enough, there was a hissing, tearing sound, and two more long black cracks appeared on the Barrier surface, running sideways from the main hole down to ground level. A sock began to ooze through one, like a striped snake. Two tennis balls popped through the other, followed by some gardening gloves and a baby's pacifier. The watching stall-holders cheered.

"You idiot, Peabody!" roared the tall Guard with the whistle. "If I've told you once, I've told you a thousand times, gently, *gently*! Look what you've done!"

Now more and more objects were popping through the holes in the Barrier. A saucepan, spoons, sunglasses, a radio, a stuffed toy, an umbrella, boxes of matches, knives, cans of food, a bar of chocolate, letters, newspapers, books . . . they fell and lay in heaps on the ground, and still more came.

"Where are those Department of Works fools?" raged the tall Guard, shaking her fists at the empty air. "Get that stuff *back*, Peabody, Moore, Nghi! Come on! The rest of you, hold back the scavengers. Hold them!" A half-eaten ham sandwich shot through the crack above her head and landed on her cap. The stall-holders, held back by a row of embarrassed-looking Guards, roared with joy.

"Who are those people?" Patrick asked Wendy, who was sniggering happily as she watched the tall Guard find the ham sandwich and throw it on the ground in disgust. "Those people she called the scavengers?"

"They're the Barrier-combers," Wendy answered. "They're like beachcombers, who collect things washed up on beaches. You have them on your side, don't you? Well, the Barrier-combers go along the Barrier picking up the things the Guards don't throw back. Then they sell them at those little stalls. You always find lots of them clustered near weak spots on the Barrier, where there are more breaks and more things to pick up. That's why there are so many just here." She looked rather affectionately at the raggedy group before them.

"They really don't do any harm, you know," she went on, smiling tolerantly. "It's only that they get a bit eager, sometimes, and some of them do try to get in under the Guards' noses and take things that really should go back. And it has been known for one or two of the old-timers to give a weak place a bit of a knock to get a Barrier break going, if things have been quiet. Very naughty. But you can understand it, I suppose, in one way. It's not much of a living, selling stuff like secondhand single socks, is it? You can understand them trying for a few things that might bring in a bit of real money. Oh, dear, look at that!"

The miserable Peabody, Moore, and Nghi were definitely losing the battle with the Barrier. They were up to their knees in household goods, food, toys, and garden tools and had by now given up even trying to put things back, concentrating all their efforts on not getting hit by the things still falling down on their heads and bouncing through the Barrier at knee level.

"You're on report, Peabody!" roared the tall Guard with the whistle. "You hopeless fool! Raymond, Watkins, get in there and help them!"

"It's her fault," said Patrick indignantly. "She should've put more of them on to help in the first place.

It was too much for three people. Why blame poor Mr. Peabody?"

Wendy shrugged. "That's Annie Fields all over," she muttered. "Worst Section Head we've ever had. Blames everybody except herself when things go wrong." She looked at Patrick. "She's the one who fired me," she said. "One little mistake, I made. One mistake in fifteen years, and she fired me." She tightened her lips and gave herself a little shake. "Oh, rats, I shouldn't be telling you all this. It's my problem, love. Forget it."

"Oi, Wendy! Wendy Minelli!" One of the Barriercombers was staring and waving. She began climbing toward them, her wild, white hair and tattered purple dress fluttering in the breeze. Over her dress she wore a green cardigan, and under it long striped socks, one red and blue, the other green and gold. Patrick looked at the green-and-gold one enviously. Except that the colors were pale, it would make a good pair with the only sweat sock he had left after last winter. He looked more closely. In fact, it was *very* like one he'd lost last winter. Could it possibly be. . . ?

"Ruby!" called Wendy. "How are you?"

"Not bad!" wheezed the old woman as she came up to them, grinning. "Not bad at all, Wendy. Can't complain. What about yourself? How're you getting on?"

"Oh, fine," nodded Wendy, smiling unconvincingly. "Ruby, this is—"

"Don't give me that!" sniffed Ruby. "You'd never be happy off the Barrier. I know you." She turned in Patrick's direction and started. "Where did you spring from?" she demanded.

"This is Patrick, Ruby. A friend of mine," said Wendy patiently.

Ruby nodded to him. "G'day," she said. "Didn't see you there." She jerked her head toward Wendy. "You know it's rot what she says about being fine, don't you?"

"Ruby. . . ." Wendy protested, but the old woman ignored her. She put a grimy hand on Patrick's arm and leaned toward him. "It's in her blood," she said loudly. "Just like it's in mine. And that's the truth. She'd never be happy off the Barrier."

"Look, Ruby. . . ." Wendy began again. But Ruby shook her head firmly.

"Annie Fields had no right to push you out, just because you made an honest mistake. It was her fault, anyway. What's she doing carrying a stupid toy round with her? She must be crazy."

"She's had it since she was a baby. She thinks it brings her good luck, or something," said Wendy. "She went crazy when she found out what I'd done with it. Now, no more, Ruby, please!" Wendy put up her hand desperately. "Not in front of Patrick."

"Why not?" grumbled Ruby defiantly. "Boy's not a baby, is he? Think it'll upset him, do you?" She peered at Patrick with watery blue eyes. "Does look a bit pale, I must say," she pronounced. "Washed out. You been sick, love? Here, have a sweetie." She dug in the pocket of her dress, pulled out a handful of small objects, and

selected from the collection something round, striped,
sticky, and covered in fluff. Patrick accepted it gingerly.
There was no way he was going to eat that. He turned
away slightly and, when Ruby switched her attention to
Wendy, shoved the revolting thing deep into his pocket.

"I just don't want to talk about it, that's all, Ruby,"
Wendy said, glancing at Patrick.

The old woman flapped her hands. "All right, all

right, don't carry on. I just don't like to see that woman getting away with it, that's all. I mean, if she's going to drop something right under a Barrier break where you're working, surely it stands to reason that you're going to think it came from the other side and push it through. I mean, it's your job, isn't it, Wendy? Or was," she added thoughtfully.

Wendy cast up her eyes in frustration. Patrick looked at Ruby, willing her to go on.

"The worst of it is, boy," she muttered to him, "that Wendy was the best Barrier Guard we ever had round here. The best. Like her father before her, and her grandma before that. I knew them both." She turned to Wendy, who was now staring sadly at the Barrier. "Must've given your dad a bit of a knock, Wendy, when you got drummed out," she said.

"Yes," Wendy answered flatly. Patrick touched her hand awkwardly.

Ruby seemed to sense that she'd gone too far. "Well," she muttered, shuffling her feet. "I'd better get back and see what I can pick up. The mob from Barrier Works will be here any second. Good to see you, Wendy!" Her brown, wrinkled face looked sad and uncertain.

There was a short silence, then Wendy turned and threw her arms around the old woman, hugging her tightly. "Good-bye, Ruby," she whispered. "I miss you all so much."

"And we miss you, love," Ruby's eyes were warm.

"And I want to tell you, Wendy," she went on rapidly, "we're looking for it. All of us. The whole section, Guards and combers both. If it comes through, we'll get it. Annie Fields said if she got it back, she'd forgive and forget, didn't she? She said she'd take you back on straightaway. Well, she might think that's a bit of a joke, but if we do find it, she'll have to stick to her word, won't she? And you never know, Wendy, do you? It might come back through. Stranger things have happened."

"Yes, they have, Ruby," Wendy said affectionately. She dropped her arms from Ruby's shoulders and smiled. "Be seeing you, then."

"Okay, love. Soon, let's hope. I heard Annie Fields was being posted up north soon. We've got to find her silly pink bunny before then, haven't we? Or you'll be out for keeps. Keep your fingers crossed."

"I will," sighed Wendy. "I will."

Suddenly Ruby cocked her head. "Here they are!" she croaked. "And here's where I leave you. Bye!" Off she bounced down the hill toward the Barrier, her purple dress flapping and her white hair flying.

"What. . . ?" Patrick stared after her. Then he too heard the siren.

"It's the Department of Barrier Works Squad," said Wendy. "Stand back, love. They don't stop for anyone, and they're coming this way."

14

Stitches in Time

Down the hill toward them roared a red truck, siren blaring. Patrick and Wendy leaped to one side just in time and it swept by them, thundering toward the Barrier.

Patrick stared after it, openmouthed. Ladders were fastened to the middle of the truck and clinging to rails on either side, grimly determined, muscles bulging under tight red overalls, were twelve of the toughest-looking women he'd ever seen.

The truck screeched to a halt beside the Barrier break, scattering Guards and Barrier-combers with equal abandon. Gray hair whipping in the wind under their yellow crash helmets, the red-overalled women sprang from their places, unloaded the ladders, and formed a tight half circle around the Barrier breaks. At a shout from the short, chunky woman who had driven the truck, each one reached into the bag she wore strapped around her waist, drew out a huge, shining needle, threaded it, and held it high. "Ready, ma'am!" they shouted in chorus.

"Bunch of show-offs," sniffed Wendy Minelli. "As if all that carrying-on is necessary. Who do they think they're impressing?"

Patrick was very impressed anyway. Kicking away the objects that were still lying on the ground under the Barrier breaks, and ignoring those still falling around them, the Squad advanced on the black cracks and began sewing furiously, some at ground level, some on ladders higher up. Guards hovered around them, pushing things through the Barrier when they got the chance, in constant danger of being pricked by one of the wicked-looking needles or having themselves sewn into the seam by mistake.

"They're so *rude*, those women," exclaimed Wendy, with feeling.

"They're good at it, though, aren't they?" Patrick was fascinated. The tears in the Barrier were shrinking fast, and you couldn't even see where they had been sewn together.

"Oh, yes, well, they'd want to be, wouldn't they?" Wendy admitted ungraciously. Then she looked at Patrick in an embarrassed way. "Well, love, I'm not the best person to ask, I suppose. Guards and Barrier Works Squads don't think much of one another, as a rule."

"There's going to be a lot of stuff left over," said

Patrick anxiously, eyeing the jumble of things still lying at the foot of the Barrier.

Wendy nodded her curly red head. "It'll be a bonanza for old Ruby and the others, all right, if Annie Fields doesn't move a bit faster," she agreed. "A real bungle, this job is."

"You'd have done it better, Wendy," Patrick said loyally.

She wrinkled her freckled nose. "Thanks, love, but don't let's talk about that. Ruby said too much. I feel like a cheat now. I know you might never get to my Find—you've got to get that Eleanor Doon woman's first, worse luck. But still. . . ."

"Oh, don't worry," said Patrick. "It's not cheating. I'd already worked out your clue. I wanted to do your Find first, because of that. And," he added shyly, "because you seemed, sort of, nicer than the others, and I wanted to help you."

Wendy looked almost shy herself and kicked at a clump of grass to hide her feelings. "Well," she said. "Let's hope you get the chance to try."

"I will," said Patrick, and meant it. No matter what the dangers, he'd decided in that moment that Wendy wasn't going to lose her chance for happiness because of him. He was going to go on with the game. He was going to find Eleanor Doon's object, and then he was going to find Annie Fields's stuffed toy so Wendy could get her job back. Lucky and Boopie and Max would think they'd tricked him into it. Well, let them. At least he knew that he was going into this with his eyes wide open. And when it was all over he'd tell them what he thought of them. If all went well. . . .

He glanced quickly at his hands. Was it his imagination, or did they look a little paler than before? His heart gave a terrific thump. "Wendy," he croaked.

She looked up. "Gosh, you look a bit tired," she said. "A bit too much excitement, maybe. Come on, let's go back to the cafeteria and I'll buy you a drink."

The girl behind the cafeteria counter took notice of Wendy, anyway, and she bought them both a lemonade. Patrick felt much better after sitting down for a while. He stole another look at his hands. Were they paler or not? Well, there was no use worrying about it. Nothing could be done until the computer was fixed. He turned anxiously to the door, and jumped. Boopie Cupid stood there, beckoning furiously, scattering yellow feathers in every direction. He and Wendy hurried over to her and she turned on her heel and took off down the corridor as fast as she could go.

"You shouldn't be talking to each other, you two!" she whispered, click-clacking along on her spiky-heeled shoes. "Just don't tell anyone, okay? Now, Wendy, could you find your way back to the studio? I have to get Patrick ready and off. We've got to hurry!"

Wendy left them with a friendly wave, and Boopie and Patrick went on. Boopie walked fast, her forehead creased in a little frown. "Here we are," she said tightly, as they reached Max's door.

"I'm sorry if we upset you," said Patrick very politely. "But we're not dishonest, you know." He put a little extra emphasis on the "we." He still felt very angry with her for not telling him about the risks he was running by playing the game.

She looked at him, puzzled, for a moment, then smiled and gave him a little hug. Her feathers tickled his nose, and he struggled not to sneeze. "Oh, sweetie pie, you haven't done anything wrong," she cried. "It's me. I'm . . . I've got a few worries at the moment, that's all." She sounded so sincere that Patrick felt a pang of doubt. Could he possibly be wrong about her? Maybe she did care about him. Maybe she couldn't tell him about the danger but was worried to death by it.

Boopie put her hand on the doorknob. "It'll all be okay," she said softly. "It has to be. Now . . ."

She flung open the door. Max was sitting hunched up over the computer. He jumped up anxiously as they came in.

"Here we are, Maxie," Boopie announced brightly. "Ready when you are!"

"Let's get on with it, then," snapped Max. "The quicker the better." He took the old beeper-brooch from Patrick and began pinning another to his T-shirt.

"Got your clue, Patrick?" asked Boopie. "Got everything, sugarplum? Remember—same clothes, same TV set, Saturday, ten o'clock, like before?"

Patrick nodded. His heart was beating violently. He

could hardly breathe. Suddenly everything was happening very fast, and he didn't feel ready.

"Watch the TV!" ordered Max grimly. "Don't move, for heaven's sake. Don't move a muscle. Right! Go!"

"Good Finding!" Boopie's voice echoed in Patrick's head, as the familiar blackness closed in around him. "We'll be waiting!"

PATRICK was kneeling by the TV set with his head in his hands when Estelle found him.

"Patrick! Oh, Patrick, what's the matter?" Her concerned face loomed over him, her hands fluttered on his shoulders.

"Oh—nothing," he mumbled. "I'm okay. I'm okay, Estelle." He scrambled awkwardly to his feet. "I . . . I must have tripped on something."

"Dear, oh, dear," moaned Estelle. "You shouldn't have been running like that, dear heart, you really shouldn't. What *am* I going to say to your mother?"

"You don't have to say anything." Patrick tried to grin, despite the wobbly feeling in his knees and the pounding in his head. "I just tripped. I'm fine now. Let's go and do your shopping now, Estelle. We'd better. It's getting late."

She looked at him doubtfully. "Well, if you're sure," she said.

Patrick looked at her kind, worried face and suddenly felt a rush of affection for her. He put his arms awkwardly around her waist. "Thanks very much for bringing me, Estelle," he said gruffly. "I'm sorry I took up your time."

A faint pink color stole across her cheeks, and she patted his shoulder. "I've got all the time in the world, dear heart," she said softly. "And I'm only too glad to spend some of it with you."

AT HOME that afternoon, Patrick locked himself in his room and worried over Eleanor Doon's clue. He couldn't make heads or tails of it.

"My first is in fur but not in fun . . ." My first what? He'd thought Clyde O'Brien's rhyme was hard, but really this was worse. Claire was in her room next door and he thought about asking her if she could help. But she was always so cranky and impatient. Dad was out, and Mum was working in the front room and wouldn't take kindly to being disturbed. And as for Danny—he'd be worse than useless. He punched his bed cover in frustration. He felt very alone.

Then there was a knock on the door. "Patrick," called Claire. "Are you in there? Can I come in?"

"Yes," he answered in surprise.

Claire wandered into the room and sat on the desk, staring out the window. "You should get a window box, Patrick," she said. "Why don't you ask Mum? It'd give you a bit of a view. It'd be nice."

Patrick nodded and looked at her curiously. It had been a long time since Claire had talked to him in a normal sort of way. Usually she ignored him, or teased him, or made smart remarks.

"What are you doing?" Claire asked. "You always seem to be stuck in your room these days. I never see you."

He shrugged.

"Patrick, is anything wrong?" Claire jumped down from the desk and came to sit beside him on the bed.

He shrugged again. "What do you care, anyway?" he mumbled, and then regretted it. Now she would go away in a huff, he thought, and it gave him a nice feeling to have her there being friendly. It reminded him of when he was smaller, and Claire was the big sister who played with him and helped him do things, as she did for Danny now.

But Claire didn't go away in a huff. She sat still and looked at her shoes. "I'm your sister," she said slowly. "I care about you. It's just—I've got my own problems, you know, and sometimes it's hard . . . really hard . . . to . . ."

Patrick looked at her in amazement. She had tears in her eyes. Her face was soft, and she looked younger—more like she used to look before she went to high school. He fidgeted uneasily. He didn't know what to do. He'd never really considered that Claire might have her own problems, with friends and schoolwork and everything, like he did. She always seemed so in control of things and so grown-up.

"Do your problems make you cranky?" he said, trying to understand.

She laughed, with the tears still in her eyes. "I suppose so," she said, and wiped her face with the backs of her hands.

There was a short silence.

"Claire," said Patrick.

"Yes?"

"If you saw a poem that said, 'My first is in fur but not in fun,/My second means just me alone,' and stuff like that, what do you reckon 'first' and 'second' would mean?" Patrick held his breath.

"That'd be a riddle, not a poem," said Claire carelessly. "They're easy, that sort. They spell out a word. 'First' means the first letter of the word. 'Second' is the second letter of the word, and so on. So in yours—what was it?"

"'My first is in fur but not in fun,'" Patrick repeated.

"Well, see, what's the only letter that *is* in 'fur' but *isn't* in 'fun'?"

Patrick thought about it. "R," he said.

"Right! So R is the first letter of the word you have to get. And you just go on like that until the word spells out. Easy!"

"Yeah!" Patrick bounced excitedly on the bed. "Thanks, Claire."

"That's okay." Claire got up and drifted to the door.

"Thanks, Claire," Patrick said again.

She turned around. "Sure you're all right?" she asked seriously. "You'd tell me, wouldn't you?"

"Don't worry," he said. "I'm fine. Don't worry."

She gave him a long look and quietly left the room. Patrick stared after her for a moment, then went and sat down at his desk to work out Eleanor Doon's clue. Soon he would know what she was seeking so desperately. And then the search for Find number two could begin.

15
The Second Find

It didn't take Patrick long to work out Eleanor Doon's riddle, thanks to Claire.

"My first is in fur but not in fun." That was *R*.

"My second means just me alone." That stumped him for a little while, but finally he realized that "I" means "me alone" and wrote that down next to *R*. Now he had *RI*.

"My third is third as well in run." The third letter in "run" was *N*. It went beside *R* and *I* "*RIN* . . .*"

"My fourth begins my saddest groan." *G* began the word "groan," so that must be it.

RING—Eleanor Doon was looking for a ring. Patrick thought of all the other rings he'd seen jammed on her fingers and made a face. You wouldn't think one more or less would make any difference. He bent over the paper again.

"I have three hearts of deepest red,/In shining gold

they make their bed." It sounded as though the ring had three red stones in it, maybe shaped like hearts, and that it was made of gold.

Patrick almost cheered. No chance this time of mistaking what the missing object was. The clue was very clear. All he had to do was track the ring down. He thought about it carefully. It wouldn't be in the ordinary sort of jewelry shop, because it wasn't new. It could be in an antique shop or secondhand shop, though. He wrote "Chestnut Tree Village Antiques" on the paper before him, and after some thought added "Red Cross shop near hospital." The ring sounded rather valuable for the Red Cross shop, but he'd better check every possibility.

Of course, the ring could belong to someone and not be in a shop at all. He wrote down "Wear beeper-brooch everywhere" on his list. That wasn't very helpful, but it was all he could think of. He had a week—a little less than a week—to track the ring down.

"I've done it before, and I can do it again," Patrick thought, chewing his thumb nervously. "I won't panic, like I did last time. I'll go slowly and steadily, and I'll find it. Even if it takes all week."

But, as it happened, it didn't take very long at all.

ON MONDAY, Patrick walked home by a very long way, so that he could cover as much ground as possible. He planned to take a different walk every morning and every afternoon. He'd persuaded Paul to take him bike-riding in the park beside the hospital on Sunday and had checked out the Red Cross secondhand shop then. But, as he'd expected, the beeper-brooch had stayed silent under his T-shirt. Tomorrow, Tuesday, Judith was taking him to Chestnut Tree Village after school. He'd try the antique shop then. He had great hopes of the antique shop. After all, Clyde O'Brien's book had been there. It was the obvious place to find valuable, secondhand things, and near to the clock, too.

Patrick walked along slowly, enjoying the sun on his face and feeling well organized and confident. He reached his own front gate.

And the beeper-brooch began to sound.

Shocked, he grabbed at it. It went on beeping shrilly through his fingers. Two women with babies in carriages passed by and looked at him curiously. Still clutching at his chest, he flung open the gate, rushed down the path to the front door, and rang the bell furiously. Then he realized that one of the women might have had the ring on her finger and ran back to the gate again.

The women had crossed the road and were moving off down the hill. One of them looked back and saw him gaping at them over the gate. She said something to her friend and they both laughed. Blushing, Patrick backed away down the path, out of sight. The beeper-brooch was still peeping away, louder than ever.

And then Estelle opened the door and it went crazy.

"Hello, dear heart," she said, from the dimness of

the hall. "What are you doing out there? Come in."
She stopped and put her head on one side to listen.
"Another car alarm going off! Aren't they a menace?"

Patrick crept closer. The beeper-brooch was jumping
against his skin. What was he going to do? He pressed
his hand firmly against it, took a deep breath, and
rushed through the doorway.

"Hi, Estelle! Back in a minute. Bathroom!" he gabbled, and brushed by her, making for the stairs.

"Patrick's home!" caroled Danny, wandering out
into the hall a second too late. "Oh—where's Patrick?"

Patrick was in the bathroom trying to gag his com-
plaining beeper-brooch with a towel. Patrick was sitting
on the edge of the bath, thinking furiously. The glimpse
of Estelle's right hand as he rushed past her had been
enough to confirm his worst fear. Estelle's ring, the ring
she'd forgotten to put on on Saturday morning and had
worried about so much, the only piece of jewelry she
had, was Eleanor Doon's missing object, and his second
Find. What on earth was he going to do now?

"Do you want another cookie, Patrick dear?" asked
Estelle. "More milk?"

"I will, I will!" Danny piped up, holding up his
plate and glass.

"No, I'm all right, thanks," Patrick mumbled. He
checked Estelle's hand again, just to be sure. Yes, there
was no doubt about it. Her ring fitted the description in
the clue exactly, except for one thing. It didn't have the

rich, glowing colors he'd imagined. The band was pale yellow instead of bright gold. The three heart-shaped stones were a rather watery pink instead of ruby red. But upstairs in the bathroom, Patrick had realized that this was the final proof that the ring came from the other side of the Barrier. Boopie's yellow feather had looked faded and cream-colored when he brought it home. The pictures in Clyde O'Brien's book had looked delicate and soft at Chestnut Tree Village but boldly colorful at "Finders Keepers." Obviously, things that crossed the Barrier didn't show their true colors.

"Patrick, you aren't feeling sick, are you, dear heart?" Estelle leaned over the kitchen table to feel his forehead. "You're a bit warm. Maybe you'd better have a little nap."

"I'm okay," said Patrick, trying to smile. He looked under his eyelashes at her hand as she drew it away. "Estelle," he went on, in what he hoped was a casual way. "You know your ring? Have you had it a long time?"

She jumped a little nervously and put her left hand over the ring, as if to protect it. "Oh . . . I don't really know. Why, Patrick?"

He shrugged and looked around the room as though he was thinking about other things. "I just wondered," he said after a moment. "You always wear it, don't you? And you were worried when you left it at home on Saturday. I just wondered . . . you know, if someone you like gave it to you, or something."

She was silent for a moment. She uncovered the ring and looked at it with a strange expression on her face. She touched the three pink hearts with a gentle

finger. "No, no one gave it to me," she said quietly. "As a matter of fact, I found it, Patrick. On the street one day. I thought it was the loveliest thing I'd ever seen. I took it to the police station, of course." She shook her head. "I was very tempted just to take it home. But then I thought, well, that's just the same as stealing, isn't it? So I did take it and hand it in. I really hated leaving it, especially as they didn't seem to think it was very valuable or anything." She sighed, looking at the ring.

"But you got it back?" asked Patrick, watching her.

"Oh, yes, I got it back. No one came and claimed it, and so in the end they said I could keep it. I was so happy! And I haven't taken it off since. I don't know why I love it so much, I really don't, Patrick." Estelle smiled at him. "Except that for some reason it seems to cheer me up. Ever since I got it, I've felt better in myself. Funny, isn't it? Silly, really." She laughed at herself, but again her left hand covered the ring protectively.

"Can I find a ring like your ring one day, Estelle?" chirped Danny, craning his neck to see it.

She laughed again. "You might, Danny. You should keep your eyes open when you walk down the street. Then you might find one."

"I do keep my eyes open," said Danny seriously. "I find things, but not rings. I found a golf ball in the park. I found half of a chocolate, but Mum said I had to throw it in the trash. Patrick. . . ." Danny tugged at his brother's sleeve. "Patrick, do you want to see my golf ball? Patrick?"

Patrick shook his head. "Not now, Danny." He slipped from his chair and walked into the living room.

"Patrick always says that," he heard Danny complain. "He always says 'not now' to me."

"Never mind." Estelle's voice was soothing. "Never

mind, little boy. Patrick's just thinking about something else at the moment. He's got something on his mind, I think. A bit of a problem. Poor Patrick."

Listening, Patrick put his head in his hands. Estelle had hit the nail on the head this time. Boy, had she ever! She sounded sorry for him. But what would she say if she knew just what his problem was? And how on earth was he ever going to solve it?

16

PATRICK'S ARGUMENT

All day Tuesday Patrick thought about Estelle and Eleanor Doon's ring. He found he was having arguments with himself about it.

"Estelle will give me the ring once I tell her it belongs to someone who wants it back," one side of his mind would say.

"No, she won't!" the other side of his mind would answer. "She loves that ring so much. She won't give it up just on your say-so, dimwit! And anyway, how could you even *think* of making poor Estelle give away something she cares about so much?"

"It doesn't really belong to her," the first side of his mind would argue. "It belongs to Eleanor Doon."

"Eleanor Doon is a horrible woman, it seems to me," his softer side would say. "And Estelle's sweet and kind."

"So what?" his other side would sneer. "The ring

belongs to Eleanor Doon. It doesn't matter what she's like. It doesn't matter what Estelle's like. It's not up to you to decide who *deserves* the ring. All you have to do is return it to its rightful owner. And go on to the third Find, for Wendy. And win the computer."

At that, the other side of his mind would pounce. "Aha! 'And win the computer'—that's the real point, isn't it? You just want to win that computer, and you don't care who you hurt to do it, isn't that right?"

"No, it isn't!"

"Yes, it is!"

"*No, it isn't!!!*"

And Patrick would grind his teeth, and push his hands through his hair, and try to forget about the whole thing. And he would try to listen to Miss Beale talking about Antarctica, or Michael going on about his dad's Porsche, or the school librarian reading aloud. But sooner or later he would find himself thinking again, and the whole argument would run itself through one more time. And there was never any real answer.

ON WEDNESDAY Patrick dragged his feet as he walked up the path to the front door. He'd started feeling guilty every time he even thought about Estelle, and he was dreading having to see her and talk to her and having to keep his eyes from straying to her thin finger where Eleanor Doon's ring sat pale and unwinking.

It was so unfair! He sat nibbling cookies in the kitchen while Danny chattered like a grubby little bird

beside him and Estelle moved around tidying up, looking kind and defenseless. Of all people, why did it have
to be Estelle he was being asked to betray? Because by
now he knew that to take the ring from her would be a
sort of betrayal. Estelle had so little. Eleanor Doon had
so much. Eleanor Doon's fingers had been crowded
with rings of every shape and size, and around her neck
gold chains threaded with shining stones had hung.
What could one little ring mean to her? But it was all
Estelle had, and it made her happy. If she lost it. . . .

He had to make up his mind. If he didn't ask Estelle
for the ring today it would be too late. She didn't have a
phone, and this was the last time he'd be seeing her this
week. He had to have the ring for Saturday morning, for
ten o'clock, for "Finders Keepers." He had to. It wasn't
just the computer. There was Wendy Minelli to think
of, too. She was depending on him to get his second
Find so he could go after hers, and help her get her job
back. Oh, what a mess! He put his face in his hands.

"Are you going to be sick, Patrick?" asked Danny
with interest, peering at him.

Estelle spun around from her work at the sink.

Patrick lifted his head and tried to smile. "I was just
thinking," he said.

"At kindergarten, when my friend Timmy put down
his head like that, he got up and was sick," said Danny.

"There's nothing wrong with me," said Patrick
firmly. He took a deep breath. "Listen, Estelle—"

"Patrick, I was wondering," said Estelle, at the same moment. They laughed and stopped.

"You first," he said. He hadn't really worked out what he was going to say, anyway.

"Well," she began, "I was wondering whether you'd like me to take you to Chestnut Tree Village again this Saturday. I'm going, to do some shopping. I just thought I'd ask, you know, to see if you. . . ." Her voice trailed off, and Patrick realized that he was staring fiercely at her.

"That'd be great, Estelle," he heard himself saying. "Thanks a lot."

"All right, then," she said, turning back to the sink. "I'll pick you up at half past eight, like last time, okay?"

Patrick nodded and watched her frail shoulders as she bent over the dishes. So Estelle had made up his mind for him. She would wear the ring to Chestnut Tree Village. She would sit down and have a coffee, like last time. All he would have to do would be to borrow the ring and get it from the coffee shop to the TV set. Then it would all be over. Simple.

Patrick sighed. It was simple. His problem was solved. He just wished he felt happier about it.

THAT night, Patrick had a very bad dream. He called out and cried in his sleep and woke sweating and terrified with Judith bending over him. "Estelle . . . Estelle. . . ." he sobbed, and Judith hugged him, and gave him a drink of water, and tried to comfort him.

"It's okay, Patrick darling, I'm here," she soothed. "Everything's okay."

"Estelle was lost," cried Patrick. "She was so scared and lost and there was a monster coming to get her.

And then I was Estelle, and the monster was going to get me, and there wasn't anywhere to hide, and. . . ."

"It was just a dream, darling. All over now." Judith rocked him in her arms. She was warm, and he could hear her heart beating under his ear. Slowly he started to calm down and relax into her arms. She turned his pillow over and laid his head down on the cool cotton. She covered him lightly with his sheet and blew softly on his hot forehead, stroking his damp hair back. "Go back to sleep now, sweetie. Everything's all right now. Do you want to go to the toilet?"

He shook his head and shut his eyes. Judith stayed beside his bed, stroking his head softly, just as she used to do when he was Danny's age and had nightmares he could never remember when morning came. He still found it very comforting. But he lay there with his eyes closed and knew that this was one nightmare he wouldn't forget. For he hadn't told Judith the really frightening part. He'd told her that in his dream he had become the lost and frightened Estelle. What he hadn't told her was that he was the monster, as well.

17

Time to Decide

On Saturday, Patrick and Estelle took the round-about bus to Chestnut Tree Village and again arrived at the escalator just as the blacksmith's clock was striking half past nine. Patrick was very quiet. He thought about how he had felt last Saturday, full of fear and excitement. How different he felt today. He had succeeded in his second Find. But it felt more like a failure than a success. He tried to focus his mind on "Finders Keepers"—on Boopie's congratulations and Wendy's relief, on the cheering audience, and on the Ezy-way computer that would soon be his. But it was no good. Estelle's trusting, friendly face kept breaking through his rosy dream and making it crumble.

"I'll have a cup of coffee at that nice café again, Patrick, all right?" asked Estelle. "And you can look around up here again—that is, if you promise not to run around like you did last time. I don't want you hurting yourself again."

"I've got some money, Estelle," said Patrick quickly. "So I can have a drink with you, if that's okay."

"That would be lovely, dear heart. Come on, then—there's a table free just near the clock."

They sat down and gave the waitress their orders.

"This is nice," sighed Estelle. "Nice to sit down— and nice to have company." She leaned back in her chair. "I don't get out much," she added. "Except to go shopping, of course, and to work."

"Why don't you?" asked Patrick, really wanting to know. If Estelle went out more, and made more friends, he thought, she wouldn't need an old ring to cheer her up.

She shrugged and took her coffee from the waitress with a timid smile. "Oh, well, you know, some people are good at that sort of thing, and some people aren't, Patrick. I don't . . . I don't seem to have the confidence, you know?" She fiddled with a paper napkin and looked embarrassed. "You're a bit young to understand what I mean, I think, dear heart," she murmured.

They drank in silence for a moment. Patrick pushed his orange juice away half-finished. His stomach was churning so much that the drink was making him feel sick.

"Don't you want to explore, like last time, Patrick?" Estelle asked, sipping at her coffee. "This is rather hot, and I'm afraid I can't drink it too quickly."

"Sure." Patrick stood up. He couldn't stand sitting there any longer, and it was still only a quarter to ten. He remembered the money in his pocket and put some on the table. "I'll leave this, just in case," he said. "I'll be back soon."

He walked away, past the clock, over to the magic shop, and pretended to be looking at the things in the window. The more time he spent with Estelle, the meaner he felt. What was he going to say to her when he got back from "Finders Keepers" without the ring? He'd planned to tell her that the lady who owned the ring came by and recognized it while he was holding it and took it back. That would be true, sort of. But now that the moment had almost arrived he could see how thin and unlikely that story seemed.

And even that wasn't the worst thing. So what if Eleanor Doon was the ring's rightful owner? On this side of the Barrier the rightful owner was Estelle. And Estelle was his friend. And he was planning to steal her treasure away from her.

It was the same old argument all over again. Patrick turned away from the magic shop's display of false beards, plastic cockroaches, and flowers that squirted water and looked back to where Estelle sat, sipping her coffee. She lifted her head and saw him, and waved.

His heart sank. He couldn't do it. He just couldn't do it to her. No prize, no promise to Wendy Minelli, *nothing* was worth hurting Estelle like that.

He put his hands in his pockets and slowly walked

back to her over the shining tiles of the plaza. Well, that was that. The game was over, for him. He hoped Wendy would understand.

IN FIVE minutes Patrick and Estelle were riding down the escalator again. Patrick looked back and sighed. He knew he'd made the right decision, but that didn't stop

him feeling depressed. He knew it was unreasonable, but he felt almost cross with Estelle, too, just for being so helpless and alone that he hated the thought of hurting her. If she'd been a different kind of person, she wouldn't have cared about the ring. Then he could have taken it, or asked for it, and bought her another one or something, and that would have been that. But oh, no. Estelle had to be the one person on this side of the Barrier who would care about a little, ordinary-looking ring she picked up on the street.

She glanced at him anxiously. "Are you all right, dear heart?" she fluttered.

"I'm fine," he answered shortly, and pretended not to see the hurt look in her eyes as she smiled and quickly faced the front again. I'm just fine, he thought, as they stepped off the escalator and he followed her to the bread shop. I've just lost a chance in a million, that's all. And Wendy's lost her chance to get her job back. And everyone at "Finders Keepers" will think I couldn't find the ring. They'll think I'm no good as a Finder. But I am good. I am!

He looked sourly at Estelle's reflection in the mirror beside the bread shop. She was so pale and sick-looking all the time. So confused and vague and sort of weak. No wonder it took so long for her to get served. She always had to wait for ages, because the people behind the counters seemed hardly to notice her, and she was too timid to call out. The woman standing next to them was crabby and weather-beaten—but at least she looked healthy. Compared with her and the other customers, Estelle looked like a sad ghost. He felt even crosser with her.

He looked at his watch. Five minutes to ten. Almost too late now to get upstairs and into the department store, even if he changed his mind.

Patrick gave himself a little shake. This was no good, thinking like this. He'd made his decision and he had to stick to it. It was probably for the best, anyway. After all, with the computer breaking down all the time there was a real risk that he'd be stuck over the Barrier for too long. And the pie-eating workman had said what that could mean. Trans Barrier Effect. He shivered at the thought.

Well, at least he'd had the experience of "Finders Keepers." And not just "Finders Keepers," either. The things he'd seen! The Barrier! He started thinking about the Barrier, and the Guards, and the terribly efficient Department of Barrier Works Squad. He thought about that boss Guard, Annie Fields, with the ham sandwich on her head, and smiled. He thought about the old Barrier-comber, Ruby, and smiled again.

"Oh, well, it's nice to see you smile, dear heart," said Estelle, beside him. "It won't be long now, I'm sure. Would you like me to buy you a doughnut? A chocolate-iced one?"

He nodded firmly. "Yes, please, Estelle." It was a way of saying sorry to her for having been unfriendly. None of this was her fault.

Estelle went back to her waiting-for-attention mode, and he let his thoughts drift back to the Barrier. Maybe old Ruby and her friends would find the chief Guard's rabbit for Wendy. It might just fall through the Barrier one fine day. It easily might. No one on this side would care about it. It'd be very pale and dull and easily over-looked. Like Clyde O'Brien's book, and Eleanor Doon's ring.

Ruby would be so happy if she found it. She obviously really liked Wendy, and she was a nice old lady, even if she did look a bit strange and her "sweeties" were old and covered in fluff. She must be shortsighted, Patrick thought, remembering how she hadn't seen him at first, even though he was standing right next to Wendy.

He remembered Ruby's watery blue eyes peering at him. She'd thought he'd been sick. Said he looked "all washed out"—and gave him the horrible candy to cheer him up. It was a wonder he wasn't sick, with all the shocks he'd been getting. He'd certainly felt strange and confused all the time he was on that side of the Barrier. Maybe that was the first sign of Trans Barrier Effect.

"Won't be long now, dear heart," whispered Estelle, as yet another person was served ahead of her. She clutched at her handbag with nervous fingers, vainly try-ing to attract the shop assistant's attention.

Patrick looked at her thoughtfully. She wasn't getting anywhere. Maybe he should try to help her get served, or they'd be stuck here all morning. He lifted up his hand and gave the shop assistant a little wave, as he'd seen his mother do. She smiled and came up to them. "You next, dear?" she said brightly, and then gave a little jump as she saw Estelle. "Oh, sorry, madam, have you been waiting long? I didn't see you there."

Patrick stared. Estelle began to stammer. The shop assistant waited impatiently. On Estelle's finger Eleanor Doon's ring gleamed dully as she fumbled in her purse. It was painful to see. Through Patrick's mind raced words and pictures. Ruby's croaking voice; himself, stumbling and confused, being teased by Lucky and comforted by Boopie; Wendy buying his lemonade; Boopie Cupid telling him not to worry, no one on his side of the Barrier would care about the missing objects. Everything he'd seen and done on "Finders Keepers."

And in a flash, he knew what he had to do. His mind was quite clear. All the arguments he'd had with himself, all his worry, just melted away. He looked at his watch. It was one minute to ten.

"Estelle," he said clearly and loudly.

She looked down at him in surprise.

"Estelle," he said. "Give me your ring to hold for a minute." He held out his hand.

She opened her mouth in confusion and began to shake her head.

"Quickly, Estelle," he said, staring straight into her eyes. "Please, give it to me quickly." He reached over and took her limp hand. He pulled the ring from her finger. He turned and ran.

18

THE SHOW MUST GO ON

"Patrick! Patrick! Wait! What are you doing? Come back!" Estelle was running after him as he darted through the staring shoppers and made for the escalator. He jumped on, gripping the ring tightly in one hand. He looked at his watch—only thirty seconds to go before ten o'clock. Would he make it? Could he possibly make it?

The escalator was crowded. He couldn't run up the steps but had to stand still and let it take him along—so slowly it seemed to him, with the seconds ebbing away. Looking back over his shoulder he could see that Estelle was on the escalator, too—down toward the bottom. She was frantically peering up, dodging her head right and left to catch a glimpse of him. He bit his lip. No time for second thoughts now.

He reached the top floor, and his feet barely touched the ground as he sprang from the escalator and began to

run across the plaza in the direction of the department
store. He glanced over his shoulder. Yes, Estelle was
just reaching the top now. She had seen him. She was
running after him. He looked at his watch—ten seconds
to go.

And then something caught him just below his
knee, and he felt himself falling, crashing to the
ground. He sprawled on the cold tiles, the burning in
his hands and his knees and the painful beating of his
heart nothing compared with the dreadful knowledge
that with every heartbeat a second was going by, and
with it his chance to make it to the TV set by ten
o'clock.

Faces swam into view above him: strange, concerned
faces, and then one familiar one. A worried, confused
face. Estelle held out her hand to him and he struggled
to get up, but his head was swimming and he fell back
on the tiles. It was then that he realized it was too late.
Time had beaten him. He looked at his watch, and just
as he did so he saw the second hand click forward to
mark ten o'clock exactly. Lucky would be calling him
now. And he wouldn't be there to answer.

Again he tried to get up, and this time he managed
it. He stood unsteadily, brushing his knees and feeling
himself grow red as the kindly faces stared. He realized
he was still holding Estelle's ring tightly in one hand.
He hadn't lost it. Well, at least that was something.

"Patrick—" Estelle was trying to speak to him. The
other people began to move back and away, seeing that

he was all right and had someone to look after him.

He took a deep breath. Now he would have to explain. Somehow. He dropped his eyes and saw what had tripped him. He'd run straight into the corner of the little white fence that surrounded the big clock. Not looking where he was going. Just like him, he thought disgustedly. He looked up to meet Estelle's sad eyes, looked away, looked up at the clock. And gasped. Its big minute hand was trembling just before the twelve. Of course. He hadn't heard it strike. He hadn't heard it strike ten.

"My watch is fast!" he yelled, and took to his heels. He'd forgotten to fix his watch this morning. In all the confusion and worry, he'd forgotten it always ran fast.

But the Chestnut Tree Village clock was never wrong.

"Patrick, where are you *going?*" screamed Estelle. She threw up her hands in despair and began to chase him again. At the entrance to the department store he turned and hesitated. She was just behind him, and the clock was beginning to whir, preparing to strike. Patrick ran on.

The TV set was there, at the end of the row. He turned to Channel 8 and crossed his fingers. Estelle was running down the aisle toward him, her wispy hair straggling out behind her, her breath coming in sobbing little gasps. The clock began to strike. One, two, three. . . .

Lucky Lamont appeared on the screen. "So, do we have a second Find, folks? Let's see! Oh, boy, this is exciting! Finder Patrick . . ."

Estelle was a few steps away. Patrick tensed all his muscles for a final effort.

"Patrick," cried Lucky. "Are you ready to go on playing 'Finders Keepers'?"

Patrick leaned out and grabbed Estelle's frail arm, pulling her toward him. He seized her in a bear hug, holding her tight. "Yes!" he yelled. "Yes!"

There was a crash, like thunder. Estelle's scream echoed in his ears as the darkness closed in.

"HAS HE got it?" Eleanor Doon was standing up in her seat, wringing her bony hands, screwing up her eyes against the flickering, blinding light that flooded Patrick,

Lucky Lamont, and Boopie Cupid. She shouted against the audience's screams of fear and excitement and against the gradually dying sound of a thunderous explosion and the whirring and popping of machinery. She seemed unaware of anything but Patrick.

Lucky was turning helplessly this way and that, his gleaming smile fixed in place, his eyes rolling. The lights were blinking weirdly, the studio crew were running around in circles, shouting at one another. But Boopie stepped quickly up to Patrick.

"Are you all right, sweetie pie?" she whispered. Her eyes were wide and frightened.

He nodded dumbly. "What . . . what," he stammered, looking helplessly around.

"I don't know what's happened," she said. "It was just as you came back. A huge bang, and everything went haywire. Something must have interfered with the transfer. Oh. . . ." She shook her head in despair, and then pulled herself together.

"I'll have to try to keep the show going, or the audience will panic," she said bravely. "Are you sure you're okay? Can you go on?" She took his arm.

Patrick nodded again, exhausted and confused. He'd been so sure. But something had gone terribly wrong. The noise, the lights . . . what had happened to the lights? What had happened to Estelle? Again he heard her scream, felt her being pulled from his arms in the rushing dark. He began to tremble.

"Have you got the thing?" asked Boopie, keeping a

tight hold on his arm. He held out his hand and unclenched his fist. A shining golden ring lay there, deep
old gold, studded with three bloodred, heart-shaped
stones. Boopie took it from him and held it out to
Lucky, tossing her head gaily and winking at the audience as if everything was quite normal. "Here we are,
Lucky," she called clearly and firmly over the continuing noise. "The second Find!"

Lucky jumped and spun around to look at her. The
audience began to quiet down, watching him.

"The second Find, Lucky," said Boopie, still in that
firm, bright voice. He nodded his head sharply and
stumbled forward. He took the ring and held it up. "Eleanor Doon. . . ." he began in a high, trembling voice,
then cleared his throat and tried again. "Eleanor Doon,
is this your missing object?"

"Yes!" Eleanor Doon pushed her way from behind
the Seekers' desk and strode toward them, to frenzied
applause from the audience. She almost grabbed the
ring from Lucky, and drew a deep, shuddering breath.
"Thank you," she said to Patrick, as though even to
speak was a struggle. Her burning gray eyes looked deep
into his, and he glanced away from her nervously.
"Thank you," she repeated. She pushed the ring onto a
long, thin finger already crowded to the knuckle with
other rings of every kind and shape. She stared at it
greedily.

"So, the collection's complete again, and Eleanor's
happy," cried Lucky. He seemed to be recovering now

that the lights had stopped flickering and the noise had died down. "Well, we're having some excitement today, aren't we, folks—a few technical hitches there, eh?— but the show must go on, Boopie, that's what I always say. How about spinning that wheel?"

"Sure, Lucky," trilled Boopie, pale under her makeup. "And let's remember that whatever Patrick wins this time, he gets that wonderful Ezy-way computer as a bonus prize!"

"That's right," answered Lucky, grinning rather wildly, Patrick thought. "Providing, Boopie, that he agrees to go on to his third Find. That was the deal, wasn't it, Pat, old son?"

"Yes," Patrick breathed. He didn't care about any of this anymore. All he could think about was Estelle and that scream that had sounded in his ears as everything went black and a sound like thunder roared. He'd caused a catastrophe at "Finders Keepers." The audience had settled down, calmed by Boopie's familiar antics. But the other people in the studio were whispering to each other and glancing around them nervously, and every now and then someone would rush across to the studio door and disappear.

He spun the wheel in a dream.

"Number twenty-seven. Twenty-seven," grinned Lucky. "Well, Boopie, what has our lucky Finder won this time?"

"Patrick has won a very valuable prize this time, Lucky. This very lovely, very old gold locket and matching chain from Old Charm Antiques," announced Boopie. The audience clapped and cheered. Boopie took a small box with a trailing "Finders Keepers" label from the nervous-looking makeup girl and held it out to Patrick. He opened it. The egg-shaped locket lay glowing inside on a bed of dark blue velvet, with its chain spilling out around it. Boopie showed him the little catch that you pushed to make the locket spring open.

"You put a picture inside, sweetie pie," she whispered, bending close to him. "The picture of the person you love best in the world."

Patrick sneezed.

"Ha, ha, ha, you're giving Pat hay fever, Boopie. Or should I say feather fever?" bellowed Lucky, laughing madly. The audience laughed with him and Boopie smiled broadly, though her eyes were anxious. Patrick closed the jewel box and pushed it deep into his pocket, out of sight.

"Well, now, Patrick—" Boopie began, as the lights began to flicker again, but Lucky interrupted her.

"Ha, ha, ha," he cackled, "feather fever—feather fever, finders feathers, ha, ha, ha. . . ." He rocked from side to side with laughter. "Feathers finders, oh, boy, this is exciting, take your chance, take your chance, let's spin the wheel, Boopie!"

"We've done that, Lucky," cried Boopie brightly, one eye on the startled audience. She put out a hand to him, but he jumped back just out of reach and stood on one leg.

"Whoops!" he cried. "He can dance, too, look at that! Time's a-wasting, whoops!" He began to hop around in a small circle, his arms flapping, jumping away from Boopie every time she made a dart for him.

Someone in the audience tittered nervously.

"Get him off!" hissed a voice from the side. Two men darted forward and grabbed Lucky Lamont by his arms. He went on flapping, and they stood there helplessly flapping with him.

Then smoke started to float from Lucky's ears, there was a loud bang, a woman started to scream, and the lights went off.

"Come on!" Boopie yelled. She grabbed Patrick and they ran for the door.

19

"That's All , Folks!"

"He's a robot!" yelled Patrick, as they burst into the darkened corridor. "A robot!"

"Of course he is, sweetie pie," said Boopie, hurrying him toward Max's room through groups of jostling, chattering people. "Hurry, Patrick, hurry! We've got to get to Max. Game's over, well and truly. We've got to get you home." Her painted lips trembled as alarm bells began sounding in rooms on either side of them and she began using her elbows to push violently through the crowd. "Lucky's had it now, anyway. Needs a total rewire, I'd say."

"But why?" Patrick still couldn't believe it.

"Well, can't you see, Patrick?" Boopie glanced at him quickly. "There's been a terrible power surge, or something. Heaven knows what caused it this time— but the machinery's going crazy. The lights have all blown and everything. Naturally, Lucky would—"

"No, no . . . I mean, why is he a *robot?*" Patrick pulled at her arm. He was exhausted, frightened, and confused. He just had to make sense of all this.

"Well, they'd never find a *person* who could do the job, would they!" Worried as she was, Boopie couldn't help laughing at this. "I mean, what human being could smile like that for hours at a time, for a start? And say the same things over and over again without cracking up? And be so nasty to people to make the audience laugh?" She stopped dead, causing two men scurrying behind them to fall over their own feet. "You don't mean to tell me they use real *people* for quizmasters over on your side!" she exclaimed, eyes wide.

Patrick shrugged helplessly. "I think they do," he said. Though when he thought about it, he wasn't absolutely sure.

"Impossible," declared Boopie firmly. She put her head down and took off again at top speed.

Patrick struggled along beside her. Then an awful thought occurred to him. "You're . . . you're not one, too, are you?" he whispered. "A robot?"

She shrieked with rather hysterical laughter. "Me? Not likely. They have to put a human minder on with the quizmaster, you know. Just in case. They're great machines, but they don't react well to stress. And when a real disaster happens, like just now. . . . Oh, thank goodness, here we are at last! . . . Maxie!" She began pounding on the green-painted door.

The door remained firmly closed, and inside there

was silence. Boopie bit at her thumb and called again. The lights in the corridor flashed and dimmed, people hurried by, and far away alarm bells went on ringing.

Patrick watched Boopie's white, set face, his heart thumping, thoughts whirling around in his head. Everything had gone wrong, and he knew it was all his fault. Trying to be clever. Thinking he'd worked it all out. But he'd messed everything up. Estelle—he screwed up his eyes, trying to banish the memory of her scream from his mind. Estelle had gone. He'd lost Estelle, maybe forever. And—it finally struck him, making his breath catch in his throat, making him understand in a flash Boopie's panic—he was lost, too. If Max's computer had broken down like everything else, he wouldn't be able to get back home for a long time. And that meant. . . . He heard again the words of the workman in the cafeteria. "Trans Barrier Effect . . . stay here too long and they're history, mate. . . . Just get more and more faded . . . no memory . . . no color. . . . In the end . . . fade away to nothing. . . ." He gave a choking cry, and just at that moment the door clicked open a little way, and Max's beady eye appeared in the crack.

"Max! Let us in! We've got to get Patrick back. Oh, Max. . . ." Boopie pushed at the door. "We've got to hurry! Before all the power goes. I couldn't stand it if . . . if it happened again. Max, what's the matter? Why don't you say something? Let us in! What's happening?"

Max opened the door a little farther and held it

tightly, his fingers white against the wood. His eyes glittered and he panted as if he'd been running. "The boy did it!" he whispered. "Massive overload, Boopie. He pulled someone through with him, Boopie. Everything's blown. I never had such a shock. Boopie, he. . . ."

"I'm sorry!" yelled Patrick, beating at the door frame with his fists and feeling the hot tears running down his cheeks. "Oh, I'm sorry. I know. I've wrecked everything. I got it wrong. I thought . . . and I tried . . . but I was wrong. And now . . . oh . . . I won't be able to get home. . . . And what's happened to her? Where is she? Where is she?"

"Thanks to you," said a familiar voice from inside the room, "she's home, dear heart."

Max stood back and the green door swung open. Through his tears Patrick saw that someone was standing there. Someone tall, yellow-haired, and blue-eyed, smiling and crying, holding out her arms. What. . . ?

"Estelle!" squealed Boopie, and she rushed forward, flinging herself into the tall woman's arms.

Patrick rubbed desperately at his blurry eyes. Boopie—and Estelle, so bright, so changed. They were clinging together, the two blond heads close, two pairs of blue eyes alight with happiness. They were so alike. How could he not have seen it before? "How—why—what—?" he stuttered. Then he shook his head. He couldn't go on.

Estelle smiled over Boopie's head and held out her

hand to him. "You brought me home, Patrick, just as you planned to do. You took the ring and ran so I'd follow you and not waste time with questions, didn't you? You worked it all out very suddenly, when it was nearly too late."

He nodded slowly. "I started thinking about how you were so pale, and people often didn't notice you. Then I thought how it was the same for me, over here. Then I thought about how you loved the ring that no one was supposed to care about on our side, and—" He stopped, suddenly remembering. "Oh, Estelle, Eleanor Doon's got your ring!" he wailed miserably.

"Dear heart, I don't care about that old ring anymore," laughed Estelle. "I must have been attracted to it then because it was part of home. Same reason I felt happy at Chestnut Tree Village, where the clock kept the Barrier thin and home was closer. I didn't realize it, because by then I'd forgotten what had happened to me, who I was, where I'd come from. TBE works on your side as well as on ours. I was just . . . fading away." She shivered slightly. Boopie moaned and clutched her more tightly.

Max cleared his throat noisily and turned his head away. "Well, that's that, then. You lot wait here, will you?" he said gruffly. "I've got to get to the studio and see what I can do for Lucky. He'll be going berserk in there. I'll be back as soon as I can. The computer's holding together at the moment, but we've got to get the boy back through the Barrier while the emergency power holds out."

"Right, Max," said Boopie. "We'll wait. Don't worry."

Max put his hand on Patrick's shoulder, gave him a surprisingly gentle pat, and then grunted and went out, closing the door behind him.

Left alone, Patrick, Boopie, and the strange, bright-eyed Estelle looked at one another. "You're Boopie's sister," said Patrick, feeling his way. "The sister who used to run the cafeteria. Who was . . . away."

"We couldn't tell anyone what really happened, Estelle," said Boopie, wiping her eyes and clinging to her sister as though she was afraid she'd disappear again. "If we had, they wouldn't have let me stay on here, and I had to stay, I had to. I had to help Max try to find you with the computer, before it was too late. It was the only way, our only chance. Oh, Estelle, I've been so miserable, so worried. We knew the TBE took months to work, but it *had* been months, and we still couldn't find you. Oh, and it was all my fault. Can you ever forgive me?"

Patrick stared. If TBE took months to work, he hadn't ever been in any real danger at all on his short trips to "Finders Keepers." Even if he'd been stuck here for days, he would have been fine. So Boopie hadn't deceived him. All her worry about time running out, her talk to Max about TBE, had been because of Estelle!

"Boopie, don't. It's all over. It wasn't your fault." Estelle shook her head.

"It *was* my fault!" said Boopie. "All my fault." She bit her lip and turned to Patrick. "It was one morning, four months ago. Estelle came in with Maxie's tea and crackers like always, and I was here, but he'd popped out. He'd left everything on, though. And I was just showing her, you know, how it all worked, and then suddenly . . . she was gone. Gone!" She put her face in her hands. "And then Maxie came back and saw what had happened—it was awful. He was frightened. Really frightened. And he did everything, he tried everything, but she was gone. Oh, I'll never forget it, Estelle. Never, never! Every night, every day, ever since, without anyone knowing, we've been trying to find you. Max has nearly killed himself trying. And time was running out. . . . We remembered that Finder who decided to stay here, years ago. What happened to him. . . ."

"Sshh!" soothed Estelle. "I came back, didn't I? Thanks to Patrick." She smiled at Patrick's bewildered face. "He ended up in the studio, as he was supposed to, and I woke up in this room with the computer shooting sparks and Max having kittens!"

"No wonder everything's gone haywire," Boopie whispered fearfully. "The system's not built for two people coming at once—and anyway, the computer hasn't been the same since . . . I did what I did four months ago. Max has covered it up, but there'd be real trouble if anyone found out." Then she threw her arms around Patrick's neck. "But, oh, sweetie pie, you clever thing. To work it all out and bring her back! Just when Max and I had nearly given up hope!"

"If you're sisters," said Patrick curiously, "why haven't you got the same last name?"

"Oh, Cupid's just my TV name, sweetie pie!" gurgled Boopie. "Good heavens, who'd have a name like Boopie Cupid in real life? That'd be *ridiculous*! Oh, where's Max? I wish he'd hurry!" She trotted to the door, opened it, and looked out.

Estelle held out her hand to Patrick again and winked. And at last Patrick's feeling of shyness at seeing her so changed, so alive, so happy, just melted away. He took the hand, stepped forward, and hugged her tight. She was still Estelle, and he loved her—on his side of the Barrier or hers.

"Come and look at this!" exclaimed Boopie, beckoning furiously.

Down the corridor moved a solemn party wheeling a long cart covered hastily with a curtain from beside Boopie's wheel. The curtain was rising and falling on either side in a regular rhythm. Max was leading the party, with a ferocious scowl on his face.

"Silly, blockheaded bundle of bolts insists on walking," he growled to Boopie out of the side of his mouth as he reached them. "I keep telling him he's flat on his back, but he won't believe me. Now, look, you wait here now. I'll be right back."

Lucky's smiling face popped out from under the sheet. "That's all, folks!" he announced to Estelle and Patrick, and giggled.

"You're telling me," said Max crossly, and the strange procession disappeared into the gloom of the long corridor.

"Dear, oh, dear," said Boopie, shaking her head. "We'll be off the air for ages. Weeks, probably. Maybe months. Still"—she brightened up—"it'll give Max a chance to get the computer absolutely fine again. And a holiday will be nice. And I wouldn't change Estelle for a million 'Finders Keepers.'"

"Excuse me—" A voice spoke from the shadows, making them all jump. "Could you tell me what's happening, Miss Cupid? Will the game be going on? I have to know. It's my only chance. Oh, Patrick, I didn't see you there. Are you. . . ?" The voice faded as Patrick, Estelle, and Boopie stared helplessly through the dimness at Wendy Minelli.

They had all forgotten about her, and now, watching the hope slowly drain from her kind, freckled face, none of them could think of a single thing to say.

20

WIN SOME,
LOSE SOME

"I'm really sorry, Wendy," said Boopie gently, breaking the awkward silence, "but I'm afraid we've had to stop the show. Lucky is . . . isn't well. And the power's failed. We're using the emergency generators now."

"Oh, yes, I see." Wendy looked down for a moment. "That's that, then."

"I'm really sorry," Boopie repeated. "It seems so unfair that you should be the one to miss out. The other two . . . well. . . ." She screwed up her face.

Wendy shrugged, and then raised her head and smiled at them. "It's not your fault, love," she said. "And that's the luck of the game, isn't it? Win some, lose some. It was worth a try, anyway."

"Maybe Ruby or one of the others will find Annie Fields's rabbit," Patrick said, slowly unpinning the used-up beeper-brooch from his chest.

"Maybe they will," Wendy answered. "And if they don't, well, it's not the end of the world, is it? I can't complain. I'm better off than poor Eleanor Doon, who only has things to love. Or that O'Brien man, who only has money. I've got a few other things that money can't buy." She leaned over and patted his arm. "And so have you, love. You go home to them, and for goodness' sake don't worry about me. You did your best."

"And a very good best it was, too," said Boopie, nodding and glancing at Estelle. "You're a champion Finder, Patrick. The best."

"Okay, okay, break it up!" Max strode up the corridor toward them and ushered them all into the little room. He grinned broadly around, looking ten years younger. "Save the celebrations, girls, we've got to get this young bloke home right now. Out of the way, Boop! And you get over there and watch the TV, son," he ordered.

Patrick did what he was told and watched Max begin to push buttons and type furiously on his computer's keyboard.

"Heavens, Max, are you doing it now?" exclaimed Boopie.

Max paused and looked up irritably. "Of course I am!" he snapped. "Didn't I tell you time was running out?"

"But we haven't said good-bye!" Boopie cried. "Hold it, just a second." She started desperately searching through the cupboard.

"Boopie!" roared Max, "we haven't got time. . . ."

Wendy stepped forward and shook Patrick's hand. "Good-bye, love," she smiled. "Take care."

"You, too," he answered. He saw Estelle come toward him, tearing a piece of paper from a little pad.

"Give this to your mum—to Judith, will you, dear heart? And you'll call home from the mall, won't you, for someone to pick you up? Don't try to take the bus by yourself," she urged. "And, Patrick—"

"These are yours, sweetie pie," puffed Boopie, descending on him, feathers flying, and pushing a plastic bag into his hands. "Not much, for all you've done, but there's nothing else here—and, oh, Patrick, you never got your computer. . . ."

"Boopie!" The computer whined over Max's roar. Patrick felt Boopie and Estelle, one on each side, hug him tightly and then jump back.

"Don't look away, son!" called Max. "Cross your fingers, all—here goes!"

Patrick felt himself begin to tremble all over. The room around him seemed to quiver, too, moving in and out of focus, from dark to light, dark to light.

He saw four figures huddled together, waving. He heard four voices.

"Take care, love."

"Go, son, go!"

"Good-bye, sweetie pie."

"Dear heart, thank you."

Then the darkness engulfed him.

◻   ◻   ◻

"You can't sleep here, mate," said the man with the department store name tag pinned neatly to his chest. He nudged Patrick gently with his foot, and then bent down to take a closer look. "Are you okay?"

"Yes," said Patrick. He clambered to his feet and stood upright, holding his head to try to stop it spinning.

"You dropped something." The man bent and picked up two brown paper packages lying on the floor beside a plastic bag. He pushed the parcels back into the bag and handed it to Patrick.

"Thanks," Patrick managed to say. He began to stumble toward the exit, trying to get his thoughts in order. He had to get to the coffee shop to meet Estelle—no, no—he shook his head impatiently—Estelle wasn't here. She was over there, over the Barrier. She was home. She was home, and happy, with Boopie and Max and the others. Now he could go home, too.

But how? He felt weak and sick. Estelle had said he should call home, but he didn't even know where to find a phone here.

Patrick's eyes filled with tears. He had used up every last bit of strength. Now he just felt tired, and alone, and very young. He looked out helplessly across the crowded plaza, clutching his plastic bag, searching the sea of faces for someone kind-looking who could help him.

And then he saw Claire. She was sitting with a group of friends outside the coffee shop. Weak with relief, he stumbled toward her. He didn't care that she might be embarrassed to be stuck suddenly with a grubby little brother. He didn't care that he was crying like a little kid. He didn't think about what her friends might say. All he thought about was that he was in trouble, and he needed her.

And that must have been all Claire thought about, too. Because as soon as she saw him, she stood up and ran over to him. She put her arms around him and she didn't look embarrassed or try to make him be quiet. And then, when he was feeling better, she wiped his face, said good-bye to her friends, and took him home.

□   □   □

PATRICK woke up in bed and blinked. It was warm and sunny in his room. He'd been sleeping in the daytime! He never did that. Then he remembered. Claire had brought him home. He'd asked her not to say she had. He didn't want his mother to be cross with Estelle. But Judith hadn't even asked about Estelle or how he'd got home. She'd taken one look at him and made him sit down on the couch. She'd washed his face and given him a drink of juice. And then he must have fallen asleep, because he didn't remember another thing. Dad must have carried him up to bed like a baby.

He looked at his watch. Three o'clock. He'd been asleep for hours. He'd missed lunch! Far away downstairs he could hear the TV. Danny's favorite video again. In Claire's room, next door, music played. He smiled. It was very good to be home.

Beside his bed, on his desk, lay the plastic bag Boopie had given him. He rolled onto his side and lazily pulled the bag toward him. He looked at the parcels inside. Both of them bore big labels: CONGRATULATIONS FROM FINDERS KEEPERS, the labels said in faded writing. There was a big, heavy one, book-shaped. He thought he knew what that was. Clyde O'Brien's bird book. Boopie must have decided that he could have it, since no one else wanted it.

The other package was a square one. He knew what that was, too. The music box.

Something hard was pushing uncomfortably into his

hip, and he dug down into his pocket. The little jewel box with its trailing "Finders Keepers" label. He'd almost forgotten about that. He pulled it out and opened it up. The little locket lay on its velvet bed, quietly gleaming. It didn't look rich and expensive anymore, but it still looked very pretty, he thought. He shut the box and slid it onto the desk with the parcels. For a moment he lay back with his hands under his head, thinking. Then he got up and pulled from the desk drawer two crumpled slips of paper and a creamy-colored feather and put them with the other things.

He put his hands on his hips and surveyed the collection. Well, he knew what he was going to do with the book, and the music box, and the locket. That left one problem.

Patrick put the jewel box into the plastic bag with the two parcels, ready to take downstairs. He put the clue-notes and the feather in his desk drawer again. They were his to keep. The sum total of his souvenirs of "Finders Keepers." No—there was one more thing. Digging right down into his jeans pocket, his fingers caught hold of a hard, sticky, round thing. Ruby's "sweetie" was still there. He laid it carefully beside the feather. Despite having gone through the washing machine at least once, it was still dirty and fluffy, but he wasn't going to throw it away, that was for sure. He picked it up and went to the bathroom to wash it. And as it began to come clean under the warm running water, Patrick stared, and then began to laugh. His last problem had just solved itself.

❑   ❑   ❑

"PATRICK, what a great old book!" said Paul, looking through *Birds of the World* with fascination. "Are you sure you want to give it to me and not keep it in your own room?"

"Oh, no, really," mumbled Patrick shyly. "You like birds, and old books—and stuff—so I thought you'd like it."

"I do like it," grinned Paul, and gave him a hug.

"I *love* my prize, Patrick!" announced Danny. He wound up the music box for the twentieth time, and the little horses began to bob up and down, around and around. He sighed with satisfaction and laid his head down on the table, to watch it from below.

"I thought he was making it up, about 'Finders Keepers'!" said Claire. "But it was true all the time. Chestnut Tree Village is always running those competitions and raffles and things. I should've realized. I didn't see any notices about it, or I would have gone in it, too. Then I could have won some prizes."

"But Patrick was the one chosen to go in it," Judith reminded her. "And by the state he was in when he got home this morning, winning the prizes wasn't so easy. Poor Estelle must have been very worried! She's so nervous." She shook her head. "And, Patrick, you've given your prizes away to Dad and Danny and me, bless your heart." She looked at her locket, gleaming in its little box, and touched it with a gentle finger.

"Oh, I know," said Claire, and was silent. Patrick could wait no longer. He dipped his hand into his pocket.

"I've got something for you, too, Claire," he said gruffly. "Not really from 'Finders Keepers'—but sort of."

He reached over and put a twist of paper in her hand. Staring, she slowly unwrapped it. Ruby's "sweetie" lay inside—newly washed, stripy-bright. Claire screamed in delight.

"My earring! My lost earring! Oh, Patrick, you darling! Oh, thank you. Where did you find it?"

"Someone else found it on the ground and gave it to me," said Patrick honestly. "I didn't realize what it was at first. Anyway, that's your present. Are you really pleased?"

"Oh, am I!" And Claire was honestly beaming.

"Patrick, this is beautiful!" said Judith, clasping the little locket around her neck.

"Whose picture are you going to put in it, Mum?" asked Claire curiously.

"Mine, mine!" shrieked Danny, ecstatically winding up his music box again.

Judith smiled.

"Whoever you love best in the world," Patrick said, looking at her. "That's who you put in a locket."

"That's right," she said. "So it'll have to be all of you, won't it? All of you, together."

21
Third Time Lucky

On Sunday morning Patrick gave Estelle's note to Judith. She frowned over it for a moment. "Oh, I can't believe it," she said finally. "Paul, Estelle's leaving us!"

"What?" Claire and Paul were all agog. "What does she say?"

"'Dear Judith,'" read Patrick's mother slowly. "'I'm sorry, but I can't look after the children after school anymore. I've been given the chance to go home. It was very sudden—I'm sorry about the short notice. I'm very happy but will miss you all more than I can say. Much love, Estelle.'" She shook her head. "I can't believe it," she repeated. "Home? Where's home?"

"A long way away, I think," said Patrick quietly.

They stared at him, and suddenly Danny started to cry. "I don't want Estelle to go," he sobbed. "She's my friend. She talks to me and makes me lovely honey cookies."

Patrick bit his lip. "I'll talk to you, Danny, and be your friend," he offered rashly. He'd probably regret this, he thought, but he couldn't bear to see the little bloke miserable. He remembered being that age. You hated changes, and people going away.

Danny looked at him doubtfully but stopped crying.

"I'll make you honey cookies, Danny," Claire volunteered heroically.

By now Danny was almost smiling. "Now?" he squeaked, striking while the iron was hot.

She grinned at him. "Okay." They began to rummage in one of the cupboards.

"Margie from the kindergarten said she'd like some work after school. Maybe she'll come," Judith said to Paul. "I'll ask her."

Paul nodded thoughtfully. He was looking at Estelle's note, turning it over in his hand. "It's scrawled, as though she was in a hurry," he said curiously. "It's very odd. Not like Estelle at all, is it?"

"Margie is nice," Danny chattered, watching Claire. He went over to Patrick and put his hand out. "Hey, Patrick, Margie is nice. She can tap-dance and do cartwheels. She's not like Estelle, but she's nice."

"Good, that's good, Danny." Patrick took the soft little hand in his and smiled. Everything was turning out all right.

"Hey, Patrick," Danny said experimentally. "Wanna see what I found at the mall?"

Patrick laughed. "Okay," he said. "Okay."

□   □   □

DANNY'S room was tidier than any of the other bedrooms because Judith always cleaned it up herself before she put Danny to bed. Patrick looked around. It was light and bright and full of Danny's bits and pieces, all lined up on shelves and clustered on his bedside table.

"See?" Danny held out a rusty horseshoe. "I found it in the gutter. Mum says it's good luck, and she'll hang it on my door. It's off a horse," he added, in case Patrick didn't know.

"That's pretty good, Danny," Patrick nodded, weighing the horseshoe in his hand and looking around the small room. Danny was a little pack rat, all right. He had quite a lot of stuff.

"Okay," said Danny, suddenly losing interest. "Let's go back and see the honey cookies now." He took the horseshoe back and put it carefully away. "Let's go, Patrick! Patrick!" He tugged at his brother's hand. "Come on! That's old stuff. Patrick?"

But Patrick was walking across the room. He was staring at something on the shelf. He was reaching up and taking the thing down. He was looking wordlessly at his brother and back at what he was holding. Then his lips began to move.

> "I'm pink and soft, with bright blue eyes,
> My ears are floppy, larger size,
> Around my neck there is a bow,
> So you can take me when you go.
> And if you pull my yellow ring,
> A song about a star I sing."

"What?" Danny bounded impatiently over to him. "That's just an old rabbit I found. A long time ago. It sings. See?" He pulled the pale yellow ring on the rabbit's tummy. "Twinkle, twinkle, little star," tinkled the rabbit.

Patrick shook his head. "It was here all the time," he whispered.

"Do you like it, Patrick?" asked Danny curiously. That was funny. Patrick hadn't seemed very interested in things like toy pink rabbits before. Patrick had certainly changed. Then Danny had an idea. "You can have the rabbit, if you like, Patrick," he offered generously. "That can be your prize for 'Finders Keepers.' Okay?" He looked at Patrick anxiously. "Okay?"

"Thanks, mate," said Patrick.

Danny was delighted. He found a sticky yellow label and made Patrick write his name on it. He stuck the label to the rabbit's furry pink back. "Now everyone knows it's yours, Patrick, and no one will steal it," he explained seriously.

"Thanks, mate," said Patrick again, gently. "You go down now. I'll be there in a minute."

When Danny had clattered down the stairs, Patrick took the rabbit to his own room. It sat on his desk looking foolishly at him, one faded pink ear flopped over one pale blue eye.

"It's too late, you silly thing," he said to it. And after a while he wandered back downstairs.

THE NEXT day was Monday. The usual morning panic was in full swing.

"Paul," Judith bellowed up the stairs. "Have you seen the car keys?"

"On the kitchen counter, Jude," roared Paul from the bathroom.

"They're not there," Judith shouted back.

In his room, Patrick grinned to himself and began putting on his shoes and socks.

"They are!" Paul called impatiently. "I put them there not three minutes ago."

"Well, they're not there now! I've looked. And I've got to get Danny to kindergarten. You must have—"

"They're there, I tell you. Look properly!"

"Oohh!!"

"I'm coming down! They're there! And if I find them, Judith, I'll. . . ."

Patrick stopped grinning and sat bolt upright. He dropped the shoe he was holding, took the pink rabbit in his hand, and shot out of his room. He overtook his father on the stairs and pulled at his arm.

"Quick, Dad! Hurry up! Quick!"

"What on earth. . . ?" Paul stumbled over the last stair. "This family . . . mad as snakes, all of you. Comes from your mother's side, you know. Patrick—stop pushing me!"

Into the kitchen—over to the cluttered counter—by now Judith was searching the top of the dresser.

"Dad, Dad—where were the keys? Where did you see them?"

"What's the *matter*, Patrick!"

"Dad, where?" Patrick was literally dancing with frustration and excitement.

"They were there. Between the milk and the kettle. Right *there*." Paul's long, brown finger planted itself firmly on the counter, to mark the spot.

And quick as a flash, before Judith had even had time to *humph* in disbelief, Patrick had hurled the faded pink rabbit, his third and last Find, at the place where the keys had been.

There was a flash and a soft, tearing sound, like a cushion ripping under the weight of a rash boy's fist. Judith gave a little scream, Paul yelled, and the milk tipped over.

And when Patrick opened his eyes—the rabbit had gone.

□   □   □

THE MILK was cleaned up, eventually. The car keys were found—near where Paul had said, under a magazine. Judith said they weren't there before. Paul said she just hadn't looked properly. The sugar bowl turned up, too. Judith had been sure she'd put it away. No one said anything about the rabbit.

Patrick wondered whether they'd seen what happened. They seemed to think the electric kettle had fused and made the flash when Paul knocked over the milk, pointing. Patrick didn't feel like trying to change their minds. Much later, he asked Paul about the glimmering specks and threads he thought he'd seen floating in the warm air of the kitchen that morning. Paul said it was the sun lighting up the specks of dust that whirled around in the air all the time, though you mostly didn't notice them. Patrick nodded and said nothing. Of course that might have been what he'd seen. But then again. . . .

He went off to school thinking of Ruby, or one of her friends, or one of the red-uniformed Barrier Guards, picking up the rabbit and hugging it in delight. It would be lying, he thought, somewhere near where Claire's earring had been found. He imagined them bearing the rabbit off in triumph to Wendy. He thought how pleased she would be. He wished he'd had time to write a note to go with it. Then he remembered Danny's yellow label. His name was on the Find! Wendy would know who had sent it, after all.

22
KEEP iN TOUCH

On the way home from school that afternoon, Patrick stood thinking for a while after Michael had turned off into his own street. Then he ran as fast as he could to the computer shop. This time the man was in a good mood and just made a funny face and shrugged when he saw Patrick slip in the doorway and make for the computer in the middle of the back wall.

Patrick played "Quest" for ten minutes and found five lots of treasure before giving up. Nothing was going to happen. He'd really known that from the beginning. He'd just felt he had to try.

He walked slowly from the shop and set off for home, not knowing if he felt sorry or glad. It wasn't as if he missed the excitement of Barrier-hopping. Far from it. He'd had enough adventure to do him for quite a while. No, he didn't miss that at all. And he didn't miss the idea of winning more prizes, either. He'd cared about the prizes at first, then other things had started to matter more.

But Boopie, Wendy—even Max . . . yes, he missed them: the people he'd got to know so well in such a little time. The people who'd been kind to him and had shared the biggest adventure of his whole life. He would have liked to see them again, to know how they were, to talk to them. And Estelle . . . it was hard to believe that Estelle had gone out of his life forever.

He began to walk toward home again. Mum would be home this afternoon. Margie, Estelle's replacement, wouldn't be starting till next week.

As he opened the front gate, he saw Danny's face peeping through the windows. The face brightened, then abruptly disappeared.

"Mum! Mum! He's here!" The high-pitched voice echoed in the hall, and running footsteps clattered to the door. Patrick grinned. What did Danny have lined up for him to do, that he'd been waiting so impatiently?

The door swung open. Danny popped out like a squeezed orange seed and grabbed him around the waist. "Patrick, Patrick, come and look!"

Judith looked excited, too. "In the kitchen!" she said. "Come on, darling. We're dying to see what it is!"

Patrick followed them in amazement. What was all this?

A big box stood on the kitchen table. A very big box, with two labels. FRAGILE read one. HANDLE WITH CARE. But it was the other label, with his address on it, that made Patrick begin to tear away the wrapping with trembling fingers. TO PATRICK, CHAMPION FINDER, it read. CONGRATULATIONS FROM FINDERS KEEPERS.

Two minutes later Patrick was staring in disbelief at his own, his very own, Ezy-way computer.

"And look at all the games!" exclaimed Judith. "Patrick, did you know this was coming? How on earth did you keep it a secret, you clever boy?"

"I didn't know," Patrick said slowly. "I don't see how. . . ." And then he realized how.

"Well, it's the strangest thing," Judith said. "Lyn down the street found it in her back garden about an hour ago. She was down there gardening, and apparently she lost her trowel—you know how you do—and she was looking all round for it, and suddenly she saw this huge box sitting under the clothesline with the sheets flapping all round it. She hadn't noticed it there before, she said, but she's terribly vague, as you know, so heaven knows how long it had been there, really. And it had our address on it. So she called me, and we brought it home. These delivery people are really hopeless, aren't they? I mean, imagine delivering something so valuable to the wrong house? And just dumping it in the garden!"

Patrick grinned. "They didn't do too badly, really," he said. He thought about Boopie, Wendy, and Estelle trying to work out exactly where the pink rabbit had fallen through the Barrier, then pushing the computer through the nearest weak spot. Old Ruby had probably helped them. They'd taken a risk. He hoped they hadn't got into trouble.

"Patrick's lucky," said Danny enviously.

"He sure is," Judith agreed. "Will you be able to use it, Patrick? It looks complicated. You don't want to break it."

"Oh, it's a bit like Michael's, and the one at school, only better," Patrick said. "I can use it." He ran a finger over the computer's gleaming light gray surface.

"And me? And me?" Danny was jumping up and down.

"Only when and if Patrick says, Danny," said Judith firmly. "And when you're a bit older."

"Aw, Mum!"

"Never mind, darling. All things come to he who waits," teased Judith cheerfully. "Have another honey cookie. Claire'll be home soon. Then we can carry all this upstairs to Patrick's room, where it belongs."

THAT night, the sound of music thudded through the wall from Claire's room, and a TV show played downstairs as Patrick sat with his fingers on the keyboard of the new computer. It was all plugged in and connected up now. He had already gone through the training program, just to satisfy Paul that he knew what he was doing, and played through a few levels of "Temple of Terror 2" with Claire looking over his shoulder. He'd discovered how to adjust the screen to maximum whiteness so that the pale printing could be clearly seen.

Now he was sitting quietly, just playing around, getting used to the idea that he had a computer at last. It had all happened so quickly. He kept thinking it just couldn't be true. But it was. The proof was there, quietly humming, in front of him. He opened his desk drawer and pulled out the white card he'd found tucked into the keyboard. He read it one more time.

Dearest Patrick,

Small pink furry item gratefully received early this morning and delivered to rightful owner, who was ecstatic and did the right thing by Wendy. Hope your prize reaches you safely. We're having to guess the exact place to put it. Ruby was a bit vague, as you got her a good one on the nose with the bunny when you threw it through. But Estelle knew your address, so we're sure it'll get to you in the end.

Love,

Boopie, Wendy, Max, and Estelle

P.S. Keep smiling, and keep in touch!

Patrick tapped the card with his fingernail and grinned. How did they think he was going to keep in touch? Hang around waiting for things to disappear and throw notes after them, he supposed. That sounded like a Boopie sort of idea. He could just hear Max snorting and saying how silly it was.

But having the computer, and their card, comforted him very much. It made him feel as though he hadn't really lost them after all.

He delved into the cardboard box of games. He still hadn't explored it properly—he'd been so eager to try "Temple of Terror." Chess, word games, "Sport 'n' Speed," "Space Cadet," "Dragon Castle"—this was great!—"Mirror Maze," "Skillmaster," "Super Punch" . . . so many of them . . . and at the bottom a small, plain box. He pulled it out and studied it. Inside was a disk simply marked FROM MAX. They must have sent him a blank one, for him to fill in himself. Or. . . .

Slowly he pulled the disk from the box. He fitted it

into the Ezy-way computer. The computer beeped and hummed. The screen darkened, and then went white. His heart began to beat faster. Then the first words appeared.

WHO ARE YOU? they demanded.

Patrick stared. PATRICK he typed slowly, and waited.

Again the computer hummed and beeped importantly, and then the words came with a rush.

WE FOUND YOU! WE KNEW WE WOULD! WE'VE BEEN WAITING. MAXIE SAID WE'D NEVER DO IT. PHOOEY TO MAXIE! SWEETIE PIE, DO YOU LIKE THE COMPUTER? MAXIE SAYS YOU CAN KEEP IN TOUCH WHENEVER YOU LIKE THIS WAY. . . . LUCKY'S STILL IN PIECES SO I'M HAVING THE BEST HOLIDAY. . . . ESTELLE SENDS HER LOVE. WENDY, TOO. HER FRIEND RUBY FOUND A DIAMOND DOG'S COLLAR YESTERDAY. SHE'S WEARING IT EVERYWHERE. CAN YOU IMAGINE? NEXT WEEK WENDY GOES BACK TO WORK—THE SAME SENTRY BOX AND EVERYTHING. SHE'S TICKLED PINK. LET US KNOW IF YOU LOSE ANYTHING. NOW WE KNOW YOUR PLACE MUST BE JUST ACROSS THE BARRIER FROM WENDY AND RUBY'S BEAT. WE'RE NEIGHBORS! WHAT FUN. . . .

Patrick sat back in his chair. He smiled broadly as he watched the screen filling up with Boopie's message. He wondered if the others would ever get a turn. He wondered if he would.

Not that it mattered. His heart felt too full, just now, for him to be able to say anything at all. He thought about Judith and Paul and Claire and Danny. He thought about Estelle and Wendy and Max and Boopie Cupid. He thought about the things he'd seen and done on their side of the Barrier and all the things still to do and see on this side. And then for some reason he thought about his friend Michael and the game they always played. "What would you do if you had a million dollars?" he imagined Michael asking.

Patrick laughed aloud. Because just now he couldn't think of one single thing.